Introduction

I'm sure countless books meticulously detail the history of the Israeli-Palestinian conflict. From every perspective and through every scenario, historians, archaeologists, opinionated scholars, Edward Said devotees and many intellectuals have much to say about this Middle Eastern conflict. However, this book is different. It doesn't aim to teach the geopolitics of the region. Instead, it emerges from the profound fracture and pain of an identity being erased by theoretical, academic self-righteousness that fails to grasp how destructive its extreme views are.

Who I Am and Why I Am Writing This Book

My name is Yamit, but most people call me Yama. My name originated from an Israeli city established in 1973 in northeastern Sinai, along the Mediterranean coast, between Rafah and El-Arish. It was planned as a regional center for the Yamit region, intending to develop a deep-water port. On April 21, 1982, as part of the Israel-Egypt peace agreement, the city was evacuated and demolished, and its residents were relocated to other areas in Israel, my parents included, so yes, I am Israeli-born and lived in Israel until I moved to the United States ten years ago.

Identity has fascinated me throughout my life—what it is, what constitutes it, and what elements shape it. As an immigrant and the daughter of immigrants, I grew up in an Israeli neighborhood where diaspora Jews were concentrated in one building. I could open my neighbor's door and hear Persian songs or go upstairs in the building to play with the daughters of neighbors who had come from Romania.

It was a wonderful childhood filled with diverse experiences, aromas, and various languages and accents. We laughed about it all, knowing we were adding something unique to our Israeli identity—something powerful, confident, and comfortable, something that never overlooked our complex and dark history and what brought us to our land, the land of Israel.

During my teenage years, tensions intensified. The 1990s were difficult times; the Intifada raged across Israel, and bus bombings became frequent. I remember being a teenager on my way to school, boarding a bus, sweating, and observing the people around me.

Perhaps someone had wires sticking out of their backpack or was sweating heavily. I couldn't endure the fear. Attacks occurred around me—the massive Dolphinarium bombing and the immense anxiety that followed. I don't think I understood then, as I do today, the depth of that hatred and the true significance of being Jewish in the Middle East.

And it never stopped—the hatred, the fear. Later, the bombings escalated into a rocket fire, and as a young mother, I had less than a minute to escape with my two children to the shelter. Sometimes, it took weeks before we could leave the house. I remember the fear at night. My body instinctively protects my little ones. To this day, even though I have lived in the United States for 10 years, every time I hear a loud noise, a fire alarm, or a motorcycle, my body is ready to run to a shelter.

Then came the disengagement when Israel withdrew from Gaza. At that time, there were numerous peace proposals, and in 2005, Israel completely withdrew from the Gaza Strip, displacing over 8,000 Israeli citizens from their homes. Israel left behind intact infrastructure, including advanced agricultural facilities valued in the millions, particularly the thriving flower industry that could have generated thousands of jobs. International donors invested $14 million in purchasing these Israeli greenhouses for

Palestinian use. Within days, many of these facilities were looted and destroyed.

The disengagement was intended as a gesture towards peace, yet rather than establishing a foundation for coexistence, Gaza became a launching pad for thousands of rockets. The Israeli government has presented multiple peace proposals over the years—in 2000 at Camp David and in 2008 under Prime Minister Olmert—offering 97% of the West Bank, shared Jerusalem, and territorial swaps. Each time, Palestinian leadership rejected these offers without exception counterproposals.

But beyond government actions, I write because I am aware of all the attempts made by private citizens, the Israeli government, and the United States. We relinquished territory and resources. Even on a personal level—rides to hospitals, education, friendships, joint exhibitions, and art projects with Palestinians—nothing changed.

I grew up believing in peace; we all did. We were hopeful; we protested with the left; we were proud and believed that we could make a change—now, I might say it was a little naïve. We followed all the peace offers with hope, only to discover that they were all rejected and were followed by more Intifada and more deaths of Jewish and Israeli families.

Sometimes, when people on social media label me a terrorist from the safety of their homes, I can't help but think—after everything we've been through, after surviving intifadas, countless terror attacks, and losing friends and family throughout the years—how did we end up being the ones blamed? It's both heartbreaking and infuriating.

But most importantly, I'm writing due to my pain following October 7th. I see that the world has faded, and hatred and antisemitism are flourishing. The Jewish-Israeli identity is being reshaped by fabricated stories and narratives, such as the claim that Jesus was Palestinian and other falsehoods that the younger generation accepts and believes.

I stayed on the sidelines, longing to scream out my pain, my truth: We tried everything. But the harsh reality is that they don't want peace; they want us to cease to exist. And this is my cry.

This book, "The Palestinian Myth," explores how the Palestinian narrative has been shaped and, in conjunction with the extreme left, seeks to undermine Jewish-Israeli identity due to power dynamics rooted in leftist theories. It strives to reclaim our narrative in a world increasingly inclined to forget who we are and our right to exist.

The Digital Echo Chamber

In today's hyper-connected world, many of us fall into a familiar pattern: scrolling endlessly through social media feeds and consuming countless fragments of information without genuinely grasping what is happening around us. This digital flood creates an illusion of awareness, often confusing us even more.

You might not realize that the content in your feed is not a random or objective selection of world events. It is carefully curated—not by editors with journalistic standards but by sophisticated algorithms designed to maximize your engagement and, in turn, your time on the platform.

How Algorithms Shape Our Reality

Research from the MIT Technology Review and Stanford University shows that social media algorithms function straightforwardly: They assess what grabs your attention and provide more of the same. A 2021 study by the Pew Research Center revealed that 64% of Americans think social media has a mostly negative impact on the country's current state, with many highlighting misinformation and echo chambers as significant concerns.

When you watch a video on a political topic, like a post about a social justice issue, or spend more time on content with a particular viewpoint, the algorithm takes note of this behavior. Within hours, your feed starts to change. Content that challenges these views gradually disappears, replaced by increasingly targeted perspectives that align with what the algorithm has decided you prefer.

Dr. Eli Pariser, who coined the term "filter bubble" in 2011, explains this phenomenon: "Your filter bubble is your own personal and unique universe of information you inhabit online. What exists in your filter bubble depends on who you are and what you do. However, you don't decide what gets included. More importantly, you don't see what gets left out."

The Psychology of Echo Chambers

Echo chambers are not just a digital phenomenon; they are psychological spaces where our existing beliefs are amplified and reinforced while contradicting viewpoints are systematically filtered out. A 2018 study published in the Proceedings of the National Academy of Sciences discovered that individuals are more likely to share information that confirms their pre-existing beliefs, and algorithms take advantage of this natural tendency.

The danger lies in how these systems create an illusion of agreement. When everything you encounter supports a specific narrative, it becomes easy to believe it represents a universal truth. This manufactured consensus is especially effective with younger users, who may lack the context or critical thinking skills to recognize when presented with a heavily filtered reality.

A 2022 report from the Center for Countering Digital Hate states that content engagement rises by as much as 70% when it aligns with users' existing viewpoints. This creates a strong incentive for platforms to deepen their perspectives instead of diversifying them.

From Digital Polarization to Real-World Consequences

The shift from digital polarization to real-world action happens gradually. What begins as algorithmic curation evolves into community reinforcement, where dissenting voices are labeled ignorant, malicious, or morally compromised. This environment can transform mainstream political positions into extreme viewpoints by highlighting only the most inflammatory examples of opposing views and Perspectives.

We've seen this pattern emerge across various social movements. During recent international conflicts, platforms like TikTok became flooded with emotionally charged, often contextually limited content that quickly sparked campus demonstrations, some of which escalated from peaceful protests into intimidation and threats.

A 2023 Anti-Defamation League survey reported an 89% increase in Jewish students feeling unsafe on campuses in the aftermath of the October 7th attacks, which correlates directly with the rise of certain narratives on social media platforms that oversimplify complex geopolitical situations.

Breaking Free from the Algorithm

Understanding how these systems work is the first step toward liberating ourselves from their influence. Engaging with information healthily necessitates intentional exposure to diverse viewpoints, critical evaluation of sources, and a willingness to engage with ideas that challenge our comfort assumptions.

The algorithm isn't inherently evil—it's a tool created to serve corporate interests by keeping users engaged. However, by acknowledging its influence, we can ensure that our understanding of complex issues isn't shaped by engagement metrics and advertising dollars but by thoughtful consideration of multiple perspectives and reliable sources of information.

As we navigate this digital landscape, we must ask ourselves: Are we shaping our opinions based on a thorough understanding of complex issues or merely mirroring the curated content that algorithms have chosen for us?

This book exists to challenge that. To shatter the illusion. To reveal how the ideas you've been led to believe are revolutionary, rebellious, or righteous are systematically implanted by oppressive regimes and organizations with dark, destructive, and even murderous intentions. It's time to ask the tough questions: Who benefits from the lies you're being told? And more importantly, what happens if you awaken?

The Vulnerable Mind: How Ideological Indoctrination Works

Young people are particularly vulnerable to ideological capture and psychological openness, which, while vital for growth and development, can be skillfully manipulated by those with specific agendas. To comprehend the current wave of campus activism and social media radicalization, we must first explore why young minds represent fertile ground for certain ideologies and how sophisticated systems exploit these innate tendencies.

The Allure of Counterculture

Young adults are developmentally primed to question authority. According to developmental psychologist Erik Erikson's stages of psychosocial development, late adolescence and early adulthood represent a crucial period for identity formation, where individuals seek to distinguish themselves from their parents and establish their unique societal roles.

This natural developmental phase creates what Dr. Jean Twenge refers to in her research on "iGen" as a "psychological opening" in which young people actively seek frameworks to understand their world.

This desire to challenge perceived norms appears in various forms: unconventional fashion choices, adoption of new linguistic patterns, or alignment with political movements that oppose mainstream values. The psychological reward is twofold: a sense of individual distinctiveness and the comfort of belonging to a like-minded community.

As Dr. Jonathan Haidt points out in "The Righteous Mind," humans are inherently group-oriented: "We evolved to live in groups that competed with other groups." This tribal psychology fosters a sense of belonging to a movement, especially one that asserts moral superiority. This allure is almost irresistible to developing minds in search of both independence and connection.

My Encounter with Ideological Capture

During my undergraduate years at Ben Gurion University, where I studied behavioral sciences, I experienced firsthand how academic environments can serve as powerful mechanisms for ideological transmission. In retrospect, what seemed like intellectual liberation was a carefully orchestrated indoctrination.

The university environment fostered a setting where certain viewpoints were not offered as perspectives for critical evaluation but instead presented as revealed truths that separated the "enlightened" from the uninformed. Every aspect of the educational experience reinforced this framework—from course materials and lecture content to more subtle social pressures.

In one particularly revealing experience, I was invited to attend what were described as "underground gatherings," spaces where the "real" intellectual work took place beyond the supposed limits of traditional academia. While these environments thrilled my younger self, they also deepened my ideological commitment through several psychological mechanisms:

1. **Exclusivity:** By positioning these spaces as accessible only to a select few, they fostered a sense of being specially chosen.
2. **Ritual:** The semi-secretive nature of these gatherings mirrored initiation rituals that enhanced group cohesion.
3. **Escalating commitment:** Each more profound step into these circles required greater alignment with the group's ideology.

I believed that intellectual awakening was a carefully constructed pathway to ideological homogeneity. The rhetoric claimed to promote critical thinking while systematically undermining true intellectual diversity by dismissing alternative viewpoints as incorrect, morally wrong, and tainted.

The Mechanics of Modern Indoctrination

Today's young activists experience a more technologically advanced version of this process. Research from the Network Contagion Research Institute shows how social media platforms act as accelerators of ideological capture, condensing what once took months in university settings into weeks or even days online.

The process typically follows a predictable pattern:

1. **Destabilization**: Young people are immersed in content highlighting injustices, generating emotional distress and a sense of moral urgency.
2. **Framework provision**: Clear, totalizing explanations that simplify complex situations into distinct moral categories are offered.
3. **Identity fusion**: The ideology becomes deeply intertwined with personal identity, creating the impression that rejecting the ideology is akin to dismissing oneself.
4. **Action requirement**: Evidence of commitment is demanded through increasingly public displays of loyalty.

Dr. Steven Hassan's BITE model (Behavior, Information, Thought, and Emotional control) offers a valuable framework for understanding how these systems operate. While they do not function as traditional cults, many ideological movements utilize similar influence techniques—controlling access to information, promoting black-and-white thinking, and eliciting strong emotional reactions that overshadow critical analysis.

The False Revolution

The profound irony of these movements is that they are portrayed as revolutionary while acting as powerful mechanisms of conformity. Young people who believe they are breaking free from societal constraints often submit to equally rigid, though different, orthodoxies.

A 2022 study by the Foundation for Individual Rights and Expression found that students across the political spectrum report self-censoring their views, with 63% indicating they fear social or academic repercussions for expressing certain viewpoints. This suggests that many campus environments have replaced one set of dogmas with another instead of fostering true intellectual liberation.

When we see students marching with symbols of extremist organizations and chanting slogans whose historical context they may not fully understand, we witness not a spontaneous moral awakening but the peak of sophisticated influence operations. These young people genuinely believe they stand for justice and liberation, unaware that their passion is channeled toward ends that may ultimately undermine the values they claim to defend.

Beyond Manipulation: Reclaiming Authentic Intellectual Freedom

Intellectual development requires exposure to diverse viewpoints, engagement with ideas without necessarily adopting them, and cultivating nuanced thinking that transcends binary categories. Educational institutions should act as environments where young minds learn how to think, not what to think.

The path forward demands several commitments:

1. Genuine intellectual diversity within educational institutions
2. Teaching students to recognize manipulation techniques

3. Creating spaces where disagreement is viewed as productive rather than threatening
4. Encouraging young people to explore primary sources and historical contexts
5. Developing the ability to maintain provisional viewpoints subject to revision

The challenge we face isn't about shielding young people from particular ideas; instead, it's about providing them with the intellectual tools to assess claims independently, recognize manipulation, and grasp the complex moral landscapes that simplistic ideological frameworks often conceal.

As someone who has traveled through ideological capture and emerged with a more nuanced understanding, I can attest that true liberation comes not from adhering to any single perspective but from developing the ability to think independently while respectfully engaging with the full spectrum of human thought.

The danger resides in the content they are exposed to and how it shapes their worldview. It's a perilous form of manipulation masquerading as empowerment, and its consequences are far-reaching. Young people who believe they are fighting for justice become pawns in a much larger game played with the future of entire nations and their lives.

 By understanding this process, we can untangle the web of deception and assist those ensnared in it to regain their critical faculties.

Cultural Blind Spots: When Western Idealism Collides with Middle Eastern Realities

There's a poignant irony in watching young people, newly independent from parental oversight, embrace causes they barely understand with an intensity bordering on religious devotion. Having lived between these worlds—born and raised in Israel before moving to the United States—I've observed this phenomenon with concern and heartbreak. The disconnect between Western idealism and Middle Eastern realities highlights a gap in knowledge and a significant cultural blind spot that distorts how many well-meaning activists perceive the complexities of the region's conflicts.

The Information Vacuum

When I scroll through my social media feeds and see college students passionately advocating for positions on Middle Eastern politics, I'm struck by how often their understanding seems to be derived from celebrities and influencers rather than thorough research. In 2023, a survey by the Media Research Center found that 67% of young adults aged 18-24 cited social media as their primary news source, with 41% explicitly stating that content from influencers shaped their political views.

The Hadid sisters—Bella and Gigi—whose Palestinian heritage has made them outspoken social media advocates exemplify this phenomenon. In a 2022 interview with Elle magazine, Bella Hadid confessed: "I'm not a politician, I'm not a historian... I speak from my heart." While her emotional connection to her heritage is valid, her platform reaches millions of impressionable followers who might confuse passionate advocacy for informed analysis.

This celebrity-driven discourse creates what media scholar Dr. Zeynep Tufekci calls "shallow information pool" environments where emotional resonance outweighs factual depth, and complex conflicts are oversimplified into moral binaries.

A study from Northwestern University revealed that social media posts about the Israeli-Palestinian conflict containing emotional language garnered 76% more engagement than those offering historical context or nuanced analysis.

The Value Abyss

Beyond the information deficit lies a more fundamental challenge: the significant difference in value systems between Western liberal democracies and numerous Middle Eastern societies. This isn't about asserting one as superior to the other but recognizing that these differences exist and deeply influence regional conflicts in ways many Western observers overlook.

Women's Rights and Gender Equality

When I was growing up in Israel, I witnessed firsthand how women's rights varied dramatically across the region. Israel has had a female Prime Minister (Golda Meir), female Supreme Court justices, and women serving in combat roles in the military. In contrast, nearby countries take significantly different approaches to gender:

- In Saudi Arabia, women were granted the right to drive only in 2018.
- In Iran, the "morality police" enforce strict dress codes, with women like Mahsa Amini dying in custody for allegedly wearing her hijab improperly.
- According to the World Economic Forum's 2023 Global Gender Gap Report, the Middle East and North Africa regions rank lowest globally for gender parity, closing only 62.6% of its gender gap

This reality creates cognitive dissonance for Western feminists who align with movements that, while opposing one perceived injustice, can sometimes embody political ideologies that fundamentally clash with gender equality. The Palestinian American journalist Rula Jebreal observed, "The challenge for Western feminists is to support Palestinian rights while also recognizing the complexity of women's rights within Palestinian society."

LGBTQ+ Rights

The gaps in LGBTQ+ rights are even more stark. A 2023 Pew Research survey found that 61% of Americans support same-sex marriage, while in many Middle Eastern countries, homosexuality remains criminalized:

- In Iran, homosexuality can be punishable by death
- In Gaza, LGBTQ+ individuals face severe persecution under Hamas rule
- According to a 2023 report by the International Lesbian, Gay, Bisexual, Trans and Intersex Association (ILGA), 11 countries in the Middle East and North Africa region still impose the death penalty or lengthy prison sentences for homosexuality

In my experience navigating these worlds, I have spoken with LGBTQ+ Palestinians who sought asylum in Israel— the only country in the region with legal protections for LGBTQ+ rights and a vibrant Pride movement. Their stories of suffering under both Hamas in Gaza and the Palestinian Authority in the West Bank present a complex narrative that rarely appears in simplified activist discourse.

Religious Pluralism

Religious freedom—a foundational Western value—varies considerably across the region. While Israel maintains religious sites that are sacred to Judaism, Christianity, and Islam (including the Al-Aqsa Mosque, the Western Wall, and the Church of the Holy Sepulchre), many neighboring states have significantly different approaches to religious pluralism:

- In Saudi Arabia, the practice of non-Muslim religions is severely restricted.
- In Iran, Baha'is endure systematic persecution.
- The U.S. Commission on International Religious Freedom's 2023 report states that religious minorities face "systematic, ongoing, and egregious violations" in several Middle Eastern countries.

Having grown up Jewish in the Middle East, I experienced firsthand the reality of being part of a religious minority in the region. The existential fears shaping Israeli policy are not abstract concepts but lived experiences rooted in both historical trauma and contemporary threats—a nuance often overlooked in Western discourse that frames the conflict solely through post-colonial theory.

Attitudes Toward Death and Martyrdom

Perhaps the most troubling aspect is the fundamentally different cultural attitude toward death and martyrdom that shapes this conflict. Western liberal values generally consider individual human life to be sacred, while some extremist ideologies in the region glorify martyrdom and exploit death.

Hamas's founding charter explicitly calls for Israel's destruction, and its leadership has repeatedly expressed willingness to sacrifice Palestinian civilian lives to achieve political objectives. Former Hamas leader Khaled Mashal stated in a 2006 interview: "The children of Palestine have nothing to lose," while current leader Yahya Sinwar has described martyrdom as "fuel for the liberation of Palestine."

This glorification of death manifests in concrete policies:

- Hamas-run schools and summer camps named after suicide bombers
- Financial incentives for families of martyrs through the Palestinian Authority's "pay-for-slay" program

- Children's television programs that glorify violence against Jews

These differences in values aren't merely academic observations; they influence the fundamental dynamics of the conflict in ways that Western activists, viewing the situation through their cultural lens, often overlook.

The Blindspot of Western Progressivism

What I find most perplexing is watching Western progressive activists, who champion causes like feminism, LGBTQ+ rights, and religious pluralism at home, align themselves with movements that openly reject these values. This cognitive dissonance reveals a form of what anthropologist Edward Said might ironically term "reverse orientalism," projecting Western values onto non-Western actors who explicitly reject them.

Dr. Mohamed Younis's research at Gallup has documented this phenomenon. He finds that many Western activists "assume a value alignment with groups they perceive as oppressed, even when those groups explicitly reject the activists' core values." This creates what he terms "moral projection"—the assumption that all oppressed groups must necessarily share Western progressive values.

I've talked with young activists and asked them how they balance their support for feminist causes with their advocacy for political movements that explicitly reject gender equality. The responses often reveal a significant cultural blind spot: "They'll become more progressive once they achieve liberation," or "It's Western imperialism to impose our values on their struggle."

These responses reveal a profound misunderstanding of the dynamics involved. They assume that illiberal values are simply a reaction to oppression rather than core ideological commitments. This patronizing perspective denies agency to the groups these activists purport to support by neglecting to take their expressed values and objectives seriously.

Behind the Veil of Campus Activism

As I watch this new wave of campus activism sweeping across colleges, what disturbs me most isn't just the profound ignorance of the history, values, and political complexities of the Middle East. What truly alarms me is the willingness of these students to justify almost anything—murder, rape, kidnapping—if it fits their carefully constructed narrative.

Their sense of moral righteousness isn't rooted in knowledge or a deep understanding; it's fueled by a desperate need to belong, to feel part of a movement that perceives what the "blind masses" cannot.

I've witnessed this firsthand during campus debates where historical facts are dismissed as "propaganda" when they challenge the prevailing narrative. In one recent forum, a student described the October 7 attacks as "complicated resistance," refusing to acknowledge the deliberate targeting of civilians, including children and the elderly.

This blind faith in their supposed moral superiority allows them to excuse the inexcusable, stripping atrocities of their true meaning. They turn even the most heinous crimes into abstract "acts of resistance" or "inevitable responses to oppression." The human cost vanishes behind a wall of ideological jargon. I recall watching a group of students cheer as a speaker described hostage-taking as a legitimate tactic, with no regard for the actual human beings—peace activists and grandparents—whose lives were violently disrupted.

What's particularly troubling is how this activism thrives in an environment intentionally cut off from opposing viewpoints. These students often refuse to engage with speakers offering different perspectives, shouting them down or demanding cancellations. They've created echo chambers where their beliefs are constantly reinforced and never questioned, making their convictions seem universal and noticeable when they are anything but.

And the most dangerous part? They don't see it. Like those who fell for deceptive ideologies throughout history, they are convinced they are the enlightened ones, the vanguard who will change the world. I've spoken with many who genuinely believe they are following in the footsteps of civil rights heroes, completely missing the moral distinctions between those movements and their current stance. They are mere pawns in a much bigger game that exploits their naivete and idealism for destructive ends.

The tragedy is that many students genuinely want to stand against injustice. Their intentions often stem from a place of authentic concern. However, their good intentions become weaponized without historical context, analytical rigor, and exposure to diverse perspectives. They end up supporting causes and tactics they would likely condemn if they truly understood the complexities involved or if the same actions were taken by those they've been taught to view as oppressors.

We need less activism and more informed activism passion guided by knowledge, moral clarity balanced with factual accuracy, and the humility to recognize that complex problems rarely have simple solutions. Until then, I fear we are witnessing not the birth of a new progressive movement but rather the recycling of old, dangerous ideologies disguised in contemporary language.

Blind Faith and Unexamined Advocacy: Lessons from "Tell Them You Love Me"

Netflix's haunting documentary "Tell Them You Love Me" presents a disturbing case study of how unwavering ideological conviction can lead to devastating consequences. The story of Anna Stubblefield—a Rutgers University philosophy professor who became sexually involved with Derrick Johnson, a nonverbal man with cerebral palsy, whom multiple expert evaluations determined had the cognitive abilities of a young child— serves as a powerful metaphor for our current moment.

Stubblefield's unwavering faith in facilitated communication (FC), a discredited method where a "facilitator" guides the hand of a disabled individual, constructed an elaborate fiction. She persuaded herself that Johnson, who couldn't speak, feed himself, or use the bathroom independently, was a brilliant poet and philosopher trapped in an uncooperative body. Despite the overwhelming scientific consensus that FC generates messages from the facilitator rather than the individual, Stubblefield remained steadfast in her belief that Johnson was conveying sophisticated thoughts, feelings, and eventually, romantic and sexual consent.

The documentary presents crucial evidence of how Stubblefield interpreted every twitch, sound, and movement from Johnson as validation of her narrative. Court testimony revealed that when independent evaluators tested Johnson's abilities without Stubblefield's "facilitation," he could not identify basic objects or answer simple yes/no questions. Yet, Stubblefield insisted he could write poetry, discuss philosophy, and consent to sexual relations.

This case exemplifies a hazardous form of projection: imposing one's desires onto a vulnerable person who cannot effectively contradict them. It was not merely a misunderstanding or a well-intentioned mistake; it represented the complete subjugation of another human being's reality to serve Stubblefield's emotional and ideological needs.

The parallels to certain forms of modern activism are striking and unsettling. We observe a similar pattern in campus movements, where complex geopolitical conflicts are simplified into oppressor/oppressed narratives, historical nuance is sacrificed for moral certainty, and the actual desires and diverse opinions of the people being "advocated for" are often overlooked when inconvenient.

Consider how some Western activists claim to represent entire populations while ignoring the diversity of views within those communities. During a recent campus demonstration, protesters shouted down a Palestinian speaker who criticized Hamas, labeling him a "collaborator" because his views didn't fit their preconceived narrative—eerily similar to how Stubblefield dismissed Johnson's family's objections as proof they "didn't understand him."

The psychology at play is nearly identical: a need to believe one has unique insight that others lack, a resistance to contrary evidence, and a tendency to simplify complex reality into a more emotionally satisfying narrative in both scenarios, the vulnerable—whether individuals with disabilities or populations caught in conflict—become props in someone else's ideological drama rather than fully autonomous beings with their intricate realities.

Stubblefield's case is so impactful as a warning because she was not malicious; she genuinely believed she was liberating Johnson. Her academic credentials, professional position, and progressive values did not shield her from a catastrophic moral error. These attributes may have reinforced her certainty that she was right while everyone else was wrong.

The documentary forces us to confront uncomfortable questions: How often do we impose our desires onto those we say we are helping? When do our ideological beliefs obscure our ability to see people as they indeed are, rather than as we wish them to be? At what point does our certainty become hazardous?

For today's young activists, Stubblefield's story should be a stark reminder that good intentions, academic credentials, and passionate convictions do not protect against causing harm. True advocacy requires ongoing self-reflection, openness to opposing evidence, and the humility to recognize that our understanding will always be limited.

Until we can question our certainties as thoroughly as we ask those of others, we risk becoming modern-day Stubblefields—confident in our righteousness while potentially harming the very individuals we claim to support.

The Seduction of Belonging: When Truth Becomes Optional

We've all felt that magnetic pull toward ideas that make us feel significant. I know I have. Something is intoxicating about aligning yourself with a cause that seems larger than life, one that promises to elevate you from an ordinary person to someone exceptional just through association. Psychologists call this phenomenon BIRGING—Basking in Reflected Glory.

I first encountered this concept in a social psychology course, and it has haunted me ever since—this realization that our identities can become so intertwined with external causes that we lose our ability to see clearly. We drop the names of celebrities we've barely met, wear merchandise from prestigious universities we didn't attend, and find subtle ways to mention our proximity to power and prestige. It's human nature—this desire to absorb significance through association.

But what happens when this deep human need for belonging intersects with movements built on selective truths?

Last month, I witnessed something that still troubles me. At a school diversity assembly in my community, a Palestinian student took center stage, a keffiyeh draped purposefully around his shoulders. His American English was flawless, and his delivery was captivating. He spoke passionately about feeling marginalized, stereotyped, and forgotten in Western society. He shared that his people's roots "stretch back thousands of years" in the region, describing a narrative of victimhood so complete and unambiguous that it left no room for nuance.

The auditorium was silent except for the occasional murmurs of agreement. I watched hundreds of students— many with little understanding of Middle Eastern history— nodding along, absorbing his words as if they were undisputed truth. Teachers stood along the walls, some with tears at this "brave" testament.

What struck me most wasn't what he said but what remained carefully unspoken. There was no mention of Hamas or Hezbollah when he loudly portrayed the war and the distraction in Gaza as coming from Israelis being evil and occupiers. There was no acknowledgment of the October 7 massacre, where over 1,200 Israeli civilians were murdered, many in their homes.

There was no reference to the hostages still held in tunnels beneath Gaza. There was no recognition of the complex web of regional politics that has trapped ordinary people— both Palestinians and Israelis—in cycles of violence for generations.

The assembly concluded with thunderous applause. Later that day, I learned something that made my blood run cold. This same student had previously faced discipline after social media posts emerged showing him celebrating the October 7 attacks, featuring party emojis alongside news reports of the massacre and posts declaring it a "day of pride."

I absorbed this knowledge while watching the school administration celebrate his speech as a triumph of inclusion. At the same time, several Jewish students had stayed home that day, as their parents voiced safety concerns after learning who would be speaking. One Jewish teacher later confided in me that she could not challenge the assembly's framing without risking professional consequences.

This is where BIRGING shifts from a harmless psychological quirk to something perilous. I did not witness a genuine exploration of complex issues; instead, it was performance activism at its most captivating. The speaker received validation for being perceived as courageous and marginalized. The audience gained the satisfaction of feeling morally enlightened by supporting what seemed to be an underdog cause. The school administration garnered progressive credentials for showcasing a "diverse voice."

Everyone got something they wanted, except the truth. I've spent weeks contemplating why this dynamic is so powerful. Why are we so eager to embrace narratives that omit essential context? Why does supporting specific causes feel so gratifying that we suspend critical thinking to maintain that feeling?

I believe the answer resides in what moral psychologist Jonathan Haidt calls "emotional intuition." We first determine what feels right and then work backward to create justifications. Few things feel more right than positioning ourselves against perceived oppression. This stance gives us immediate moral currency in a world where traditional sources of meaning have diminished.

This issue isn't exclusive to Palestinian advocacy—it happens across the political spectrum. However, the substantial gap between the promoted narrative and the verifiable reality renders this situation concerning.

When a student who celebrated the murder of civilians can successfully portray himself as the victim while the actual victims remain invisible, something fundamental is broken in our discourse. When an educational institution responsible for developing critical thinking enables this distortion, we're witnessing more than just bias; we're observing the systematic dismantling of truth as a shared value.

True solidarity requires the courage to embrace complexity and recognize that no one has a monopoly on victimhood or blame. It calls on us to resist the tempting allure of simplistic narratives that give us a sense of righteousness while asking nothing from us but performative outrage.

Perhaps the most uncomfortable truth is that genuine understanding cannot be achieved through BIRGING. It cannot be found by basking in the reflected glory of causes we barely comprehend. Instead, it arises from the patient, unglamorous work of engaging with contradictory perspectives and resisting the seduction of morality certainty.

We must consider whether truth holds more value than belonging and whether we are willing to stand apart from the crowd when the desire for inclusion jeopardizes our integrity.

When Independent Thought Becomes Extinct

I've always found refuge in independent bookstores. Since childhood, they have represented sacred spaces where ideas flourish, mainstream narratives can be challenged, and the curious and questioning can discover unexpected wisdom on dusty shelves. My good friend, a literature professor with an almost religious devotion to small bookshops, instilled this reverence in me. "Chain stores sell books," he would say, running his fingers along spines in some hidden gem we'd discovered. "Independent stores curate knowledge."

That belief—that independent bookstores symbolize intellectual freedom and diverse ideas—remained unshaken for most of my life until that Saturday.

It was one of those perfect New England afternoons that makes you forget how harsh Boston winters can be. The air carried the first hint of autumn, and I found myself wandering through Jamaica Plain, a neighborhood that proudly showcases its hipster vibe. Artisanal coffee shops, thrift stores, and local art galleries line its streets—a testament to its commitment to independent businesses and creative expression.

When I spotted a small bookstore between a cozy coffee shop and a second-hand store, I felt like I had stumbled upon a treasure. However, as soon as I stepped inside, my excitement shifted to unease. At the entrance stood what I can only describe as a shrine—not to literature or diverse thought, but to a singular political perspective. A carefully arranged display was dedicated exclusively to anti-Israel literature. This wasn't merely a collection of books critical of Israeli policy (which would be legitimate).

This was something different, something intentional and unsettling. Among the carefully chosen titles were graphic novels illustrating Jews with exaggerated features—hooked noses, bloodied hands, and malevolent expressions reminiscent of Nazi propaganda from the 1930s.

Books with titles like "Israel: An Apartheid State" and "Zionism: The Real Terrorism" were prominently displayed at eye level. Dominating the center of the display was Rashid Khalidi's "The Hundred Years' War on Palestine," presented not as one viewpoint among many but as the absolute, unchallenged truth.

I'm familiar with Khalidi's work. His credentials as a professor of Middle Eastern Studies at Columbia are impressive. However, his scholarship has faced significant criticism from historians across the political spectrum for its selective use of evidence and revisionist approach. What troubled me wasn't that his book was being sold—it was that it was presented as uncontested historical fact rather than what it truly is: a highly politicized interpretation of complex events.

For context, Khalidi's work contains several fundamental distortions that undermine its reliability as a historical source:

First, Khalidi constructs a narrative of Palestinian national identity that predates Zionism, claiming an unbroken lineage stretching back centuries. However, primary sources from the Ottoman period present a different perspective. Before the 20th century, the term "Palestinian" primarily referred to Jews living in the region.

Ottoman census records, which meticulously documented demographic information, indicate that the local Arab population typically identified as Southern Syrians, Arabs, or by their religious or clan affiliations—not as "Palestinians."

This isn't just my opinion. Historian Rashid Khalidi, ironically a distant relative of the author, acknowledged in earlier, more scholarly work that "Palestinian identity emerged in response to the challenge of Zionism." The first Arabic newspaper in the region, Falastin, founded in 1911, was run by Syrian nationalists who opposed both Zionism and Palestinian nationalism, viewing the latter as a divisive force within the more incredible Arab world.

Furthermore, Khalidi deliberately overlooks the Jewish historical connection to the land. Over thousands of years, archaeological evidence—from the Dead Sea Scrolls to Roman-era synagogues to Ottoman tax records—documents a continuous Jewish presence and cultural attachment to the region. This evidence is not disputed among serious archaeologists or historians, regardless of their political beliefs.

Khalidi also presents a selective economic history, attributing the development of pre-1948 Palestine solely to Arab inhabitants while overlooking the documented influence of Jewish immigration on the region. Development. Records from the British Mandate during the 1920s and 1930s indicate that Jewish settlement stimulated significant economic growth, which in turn attracted a considerable amount of Arab immigration to the area—a fact that was acknowledged even by Arab leaders of that period. In a 1937 statement to the Peel Commission, Syrian leader Auni Bey Abdul-Hadi noted, "There is no such country as Palestine... Syria, of which Palestine is a southern part, has nothing to do with the Jews."

Perhaps most troubling is Khalidi's systematic downplaying of the Arab leadership's rejection of partition plans and peace offers. He scarcely notes that the Mufti of Jerusalem, Haj Amin al-Husseini, collaborated with Nazi Germany, meeting personally with Hitler in 1941 to discuss bringing the Final Solution to the Middle East.

 Contemporaneous records, including transcripts of their meeting, document Husseini's enthusiastic support for Nazi antisemitism and his efforts to prevent Jewish refugees from escaping Europe.

The bookstore's display failed to capture this complex history. Not a single work that presented Israeli viewpoints, Jewish historical accounts, or even widely accepted historical scholarship was included alongside Khalidi's narrative. This wasn't curation; it was indoctrination.

I wanted to give the bookstore the benefit of the doubt. Perhaps this was simply an oversight—enthusiasm for one perspective without acknowledging the importance of balance. So, I approached the clerk, a young woman with blue hair and wire-rimmed glasses, arranging a stack of poetry books.

"Excuse me," I began, keeping my tone curious rather than confrontational. You have an entire display dedicated to one perspective on the Israeli-Palestinian conflict. Do you carry any books that offer Israeli or Jewish viewpoints as well?"

She looked up, her expression changing from customer-service friendliness to something more intense. A smirk appeared at the corner of her mouth.

"Well," she said dismissively, "When you have your bookstore, you can carry whatever books you like."

The response shocked me. Not because it was hostile (though it was), but because it exposed something fundamental about what this "independent" bookstore truly represented. It wasn't about independent thought at all. It wasn't about exploring diverse perspectives or challenging dominant narratives. It was about replacing one orthodox view with another—and defending that new orthodoxy just as rigidly as any mainstream bookstore might uphold bestseller lists.

"I understand you can stock whatever you choose," I replied. "But I'm surprised that a store calling itself Independent Books would present only one side of such a complex issue. Some of these books contain historical inaccuracies and antisemitic sentiments." imagery.

Her eyes narrowed. "I haven't even read these books," she replied, a hint of defiance in her voice. "Can you show me one antisemitic passage? Point out exactly where the antisemitism is."

The burden of proof had suddenly shifted to me. It wasn't sufficient that a display prominently featured books denying Israel's right to exist or that graphic illustrations portrayed Jews with classic antisemitic characteristics. I was now expected to provide a detailed line-by-line analysis to justify my discomfort.

This exchange signifies something much more insidious than the flawed judgment of a single bookstore. It illustrates a pattern becoming increasingly common in intellectual spaces throughout the West, where "independent" thinking has begun to signify conformity to a different orthodoxy rather than true intellectual diversity.

At universities, the same dynamics occur. Students arrive with minimal historical knowledge but quickly embrace oversimplified narratives that interpret complex conflicts in black-and-white terms. Faculty members who present evidence contradicting these narratives often find themselves marginalized, with their research dismissed not for scholarly reasons but for ideological ones.

Media outlets, particularly those labeling themselves as "alternative" to mainstream sources, often replicate the same problem in reverse—rejecting one set of biases only to uncritically embrace another. The result isn't increased truth but rather different lies.

Even in artistic communities, where creative freedom should be cherished, there is growing pressure to align with specific political viewpoints—not because they are correct, but because they signify membership in the appropriate group. Artists who challenge these new orthodoxies find themselves excluded from galleries, readings, and exhibitions, much like those who opposed different orthodoxies in past eras.

That afternoon, in Jamaica Plain, I wasn't merely witnessing poor curation; I was observing a microcosm of a much larger issue: the replacement of independent thought with fashionable conformity, the replacement of critical inquiry with virtue signaling, and the transformation of spaces intended for intellectual exploration into echo chambers that reinforce existing biases.

This isn't just about a single bookstore or a particular political issue. It's about what happens when our cultural institutions, from universities to media outlets to small bookstores in progressive neighborhoods, forsake their commitment to truth for ideological comfort. When they value belonging over honesty. When they sacrifice intellectual integrity on the altar of tribal loyalty.

The true tragedy is that none of this benefits the Palestinians or Israelis. It doesn't promote peace, justice, or reconciliation. Instead, it deepens narratives that render complex solutions unattainable. It converts real individuals with genuine suffering into symbols in someone else's identity project.

In a world increasingly divided by competing certainties, perhaps the most radical act isn't choosing the right side but insisting that truth is always more complex than any narrative can capture. True independence means having the courage to question the orthodoxies we oppose and those we're tempted to embrace.

The Battle for Consciousness – How the West Is Losing Its Way

We are not losing this war due to a lack of facts. We are losing because the other side controls the platforms that shape public opinion.

And this presents the real danger to the West:

◆ A generation that confuses ignorance with moral superiority.

◆ A media landscape that portrays one-sided narratives as absolute truth.

◆ A society that values emotional appeals more than historical reality.

Next time you enter a bookstore, a university, or a lecture hall, pause and ask yourself:
Who decides which voices are heard and which are silenced?
Who determines which books receive the spotlight and which are erased?
And most importantly—

Who benefits from your ignorance?

It's a straightforward question that gets to the core of the world's most significant conflicts: Who profits from the ignorance of the progressive left? Who benefits when privileged Westerners—safe in their coffee shops, bookstores, and ivory towers—blindly repeat slogans about "resistance," "decolonization," and "justice for Palestine" without understanding the deeper, historical, and financial realities involved?

The answer is both evident and deeply unsettling: Terrorist leaders, corrupt elites, and those aiming to establish Islamist rule worldwide.

Follow the Money: The West's Billions to Gaza

For decades, Western nations—especially the U.S. and Europe—have invested billions of dollars in Gaza under the pretense of "humanitarian aid" and "reconstruction." The figures are staggering:

- Between 1993 and 2020, international donors pledged over $40 billion to the Palestinian Authority (PA) and later to Gaza.
- The EU alone has sent more than €10 billion since 2007.
- Qatar regularly transfers hundreds of millions of dollars directly into Hamas-controlled Gaza.
- The UN funnels millions annually through agencies like UNRWA, which has been caught time and time again collaborating with Hamas.

And what has been the result? Have these funds been used to build hospitals, universities, or infrastructure for the Palestinian people? No. Instead, these billions have encouraged terror, corruption, and the extravagant lifestyles of a privileged few at the top.

Yasser Arafat: The Billionaire "Freedom Fighter"

One of the clearest examples of this theft is Yasser Arafat, the so-called leader of Palestinian "liberation." While he preached "resistance," he accumulated a personal fortune estimated at over $1.3 billion. His widow, Suha Arafat, now leads a lavish life in Paris, owning multimillion-dollar properties and enjoying a lifestyle that starkly contrasts with the poverty faced by ordinary Palestinians.

His daughter, Zahwa Arafat, inherited millions and now lives as a wealthy real estate mogul in France. Meanwhile, the Palestinian people continue to suffer from economic hardship, their lives dominated by the very leaders who profess to fight for their "freedom." So, who benefits from your ignorance? Suha Arafat, her billionaire daughter, and every corrupt official who exploits the Palestinian cause for personal gain.

Hamas Leaders: The Millionaire Terrorists

If you believe Arafat's corruption ended with his death, reconsider. Hamas—a terrorist organization posing as a resistance movement—has mastered the art of profiting from war while keeping its people in misery.

Hamas's leader, Ismail Haniyeh, has over $4 billion net worth. He spends most of his time in five-star hotels in Turkey and Qatar, far removed from the suffering of the Gazan people.

Khaled Mashal, another senior Hamas official, is worth at least $2.6 billion. He resides in a luxurious villa in Doha, surrounded by opulence, and communicates with Jihad from a distance.

Mohammed Deif, Hamas' military commander, directs rocket attacks on Israel from the comfort of his heavily fortified mansion.

Meanwhile, the average Palestinian in Gaza lives on less than five dollars a day. So, who benefits from your ignorance? The Hamas elites sip cocktails in Doha while persuading Western progressives that they are "freedom fighters."

The Money Doesn't Go to the People—It Funds Terror

If a small portion of the billions sent to Gaza had been allocated to its residents, it could have developed into a thriving economy. Instead, Hamas uses foreign aid to:

✓ Construct underground tunnels instead of schools.

✓ Buy rockets instead of medicine.

✓ Provide "martyr salaries" to families of terrorists instead of investing in job creation.

For every progressive activist who believes they are "standing with Palestine" by condemning Israel, they are aligning themselves with Hamas's leadership, which is not interested in peace and only seeks to prolong the conflict that fills their coffers accounts.

Mahmoud Abbas, aka Abu Mazen, has been a prominent figure in Palestinian politics for decades. Born in 1935 in Safed, he succeeded Yasser Arafat and has served as the President of the Palestinian Authority since 2005. Abbas was a key architect of the Oslo Accords and is viewed internationally as a strong advocate for the two-state solution, promoting peaceful negotiations with Israel.

However, there have been instances where Abbas's statements in Arabic have raised questions about his commitment to peace. Critics highlight occasions when his rhetoric contradicts his public stance on non-violence. For instance, during a speech at the United Nations, Abbas described Israeli policies as "genocide" and hailed Palestinian "martyrs" and prisoners, referring to them as heroes, which drew applause from the audience.

Discrepancies in Abbas's statements across different languages have sparked debates about his true intentions and the authenticity of his commitment to the peace process. These contrasting narratives highlight the difficulties in assessing the motives of political leaders in deeply entrenched conflicts.

They also emphasize the importance of examining statements made in different contexts and languages to fully understand a leader's position and the potential implications for peace efforts.

The Bigger Picture: Islamist Expansion and the Caliphate Dream

The roots of corruption and conflict extend well beyond the borders of Gaza, highlighting the broader ambitions of radical Islamist forces aiming to establish a global caliphate governed by Sharia law. Central to this effort is Iran, a nation whose trajectory changed dramatically after 1979, when the Islamic Revolution transformed it from a modern, secular society into a theocratic state.

Iran: From Modern Nation to Theocratic Nightmare

Before the 1979 revolution, Iran flourished as a progressive nation known for its secular governance, vibrant culture, and commitment to modernization. Women confidently wore Western attire, pursued higher education, and enjoyed rights that elevated their societal standing. Tehran became a cosmopolitan center, strengthening ties with Western nations and showcasing the country's progressive values.

However, the rise of Ayatollah Khomeini signaled a disastrous shift. The establishment of a rigid Islamic regime marked the beginning of widespread repression. Women encountered severe limitations on their rights; the enforcement of the hijab became compulsory, and educational and employment opportunities decreased. Khomeini's revolutionary ideology introduced a cruel system of oppression aimed at political dissenters, with executions and imprisonments becoming routine.

More insidiously, the regime's ambitions reached beyond national borders, aiming to spread its radical beliefs and ideologies worldwide, thus igniting global Islamist terrorism.

The Iranian leadership views the transformation of the West as critical, seeing it as a target ripe for ideological warfare.

They depict Western society as morally decaying and decadent, framing their vision of an Islamic global order as a necessary solution. Iran's modus operandi includes funding and supporting militant factions like Hamas, Hezbollah, and the Houthis—not out of genuine concern for regional stability or Palestinian rights but rather as a strategic calculation to challenge Western dominance. These groups serve as proxies to spread radical Islamic ideologies, incite violence, and destabilize critical regions, ultimately undermining Western influence.

Iran's ambitions extend well beyond the Middle East; its ideological assault on the West plays out internationally. The regime uses militant support to sustain a climate of unrest, enabling it to exert influence and impose radical beliefs. The Palestinian cause, often used as a rallying cry, serves a dual purpose: justifying its activities while distracting Western powers from the broader strategic objectives at play. Through militant organizations like Hamas, Iran promotes hatred and violence, seeking to elevate a vision of pan-Islamic unity under a caliphate.

The encroachment of radical Islam in Western societies reflects Iran's long-term strategy, driven by mosque conversions and initiatives that challenge Western norms. In various European contexts, radicalized factions are emerging, posing challenges to the principles of democracy and secularism while further complicating community dynamics and structures.

The implications are profound: the Iranian regime's agenda goes beyond mere rhetoric about civil rights; it embodies an ideological struggle aimed at dismantling the foundations of democratic values and freedoms. Ignoring the multifaceted threat posed by Iran—both in the Middle East and beyond—would be a serious miscalculation. Their strategic support for terrorist networks represents a key aspect of a larger plan to reshape the world according to a radical Islamic vision.

Recognizing and addressing this threat is essential for preserving democratic integrity and the core values that define Western society.

The Muslim Brotherhood: Architects of Global Jihad

The Muslim Brotherhood, an influential and complex organization, represents not just an abstract ideological movement but the very backbone of various groups aiming to establish a global Islamic state, including Hamas. Rather than operating as a standalone entity, Hamas acts as a significant branch of this broader network, engaging in political and militant actions driven by the Brotherhood's ambitions.

The Brotherhood has historically orchestrated the overthrow of secular Arab regimes, as exemplified by its role in Egypt's 2011 revolution. Its ideological influence extends even to extremist factions like ISIS and Al-Qaeda, both of which share a vision of a global caliphate. The core of their ideology is the goal of enforcing Sharia law on a worldwide scale—a dream that threatens individual liberties and democratic values principles.

Many in the West who see Hamas as simply a "resistance movement" overlook the radical ideology that aims to erode rights and freedoms for countless individuals. By supporting such entities, they unwittingly endorse an agenda that undermines the very values they cherish.

Who Gains from Ignorance?

While residents of Gaza suffer, Hamas leaders often live in luxury, disconnected from the struggles faced by the people. This disparity reveals the hypocrisy in leadership that sustains conflict while reaping its benefits. Furthermore, entities such as Iran's ruling ayatollahs fund terrorism overseas while systematically oppressing their citizens.

The Muslim Brotherhood's broader goal is to build an Islamic empire defined by the oppression of women, minorities, and non-Muslims. At the same time, Western politicians and media outlets capitalize on sustaining a selective narrative, benefiting from public ignorance about these complex geopolitical realities.

Every time an unwitting progressive pushes a "Free Palestine" slogan, they may find themselves not as champions of liberation but as inadvertent enablers of oppressive regimes. The question lingers: When will they awaken to the nuances of their advocacy?

Exploitation of Global Ignorance

A closer examination of the complexities of global politics reveals that various entities exploit widespread ignorance, particularly in progressive circles. Countries like Qatar and Iran adeptly navigate these waters to promote their agendas, often conflicting with the very principles upheld by these movements.

Qatar's Strategic Financial Influence

Between 2001 and 2021, Qatar invested around $4.7 billion in American higher education. Although these investments are said to support research in medicine and cybersecurity, their implications raise serious concerns about foreign influence on academic discourse and curriculum development.

Critics argue that these contributions often come with strings attached, promoting narratives that align with Qatar's political interests—including those that may foster anti-Israel and anti-Jewish sentiments. A report by the Institute for the Study of Global Antisemitism and Policy (ISGAP) warns that Qatar's financial ties to U.S.

universities could potentially shape campus narratives in a way that critiques Western policies.

Moreover, investigations indicate that Qatar's funding also extends to orchestrating pro-Palestinian protests on American campuses. Organizations financed by Qatar play a vital role in promoting ideologies that align with Islamist perspectives, connecting with various student groups actively engaged in demonstrations.

For instance, the organization American Muslims for Palestine (AMP), which has received funding linked to Qatar, provides grants to pro-Palestinian groups on college campuses. These grants, typically ranging from $500 to $2,000, support events that emphasize anti-Israel rhetoric and correspond with Qatar's geopolitical interests narratives.

Through this strategic funding, Qatar aims to shape academic and public opinion in the U.S., guiding perceptions toward its foreign policy goals and contesting Western ideologies.

In conclusion, Qatar's substantial investments in American higher education and student activism highlight a deliberate effort to exert foreign influence on academic and political discourse. By promoting specific political agendas through financial support, Qatar aims to shape public perception in line with its broader strategic goals, potentially undermining academic integrity and the balanced discourse process.

Beneficiaries of Ignorance

In the current geopolitical landscape, the persistence of ignorance in certain progressive circles unintentionally benefits state actors with ulterior motives. By not critically examining the sources and implications of their support for various movements, individuals and institutions may unwittingly align themselves with the narratives promoted by nations like Qatar and Iran.

This lack of inquiry enables these regimes to manipulate public opinion, fund extremist activities, and undermine democratic values—all disguised as cultural or educational exchanges. Adopting a discerning approach when engaging in international partnerships or supporting movements is essential.

Gaining a deeper understanding of who benefits from ignorance can shed light on the complex relationship between well-meaning activism and the geopolitical strategies of nations attempting to further their interests, often at the expense of global peace and security.

This critical examination raises essential questions: Why, for instance, did such intense global outrage erupt after the October 7 attacks? Why do we witness unprecedented demonstrations on progressive campuses like Harvard and Columbia, while similar atrocities in Syria, Yemen, Sudan, and even the ongoing conflict in Ukraine elicit comparatively muted responses?

As a resident of Boston, I witnessed an unsettling reality unfold in the weeks following October 7. Walking through Harvard University—one of America's most prestigious institutions—I encountered a disturbing scene that contradicted my long-held beliefs about higher education. Students were draped in keffiyehs, rallying in support of Hamas, shouting slogans, and brandishing signs with fervent hostility.

I felt their piercing stares as I walked through the campus, dressed in the Israeli and American flags. The animosity directed at me was palpable—some students pointed, others shouted insults, while a few made threatening gestures, as if enacting a grim scene of violence.

One student roughly pushed me aside, and another waved a finger in a mocking salute, portraying my presence as an insult.

In that moment, overwhelmed with emotion, I grappled with a profound and unsettling question: Why such animosity? These students did not know me, nor did they understand my family history or the complexities of the Middle East. Yet, here they were, celebrating an organization responsible for the most heinous massacre of Jews since the Holocaust.

My view of American universities as advocates for critical thought and moral clarity shattered in the face of such unabashed hatred—hatred directed at Israel, at Jews, and at anyone who dared to oppose terror. Alarmingly, this hostility did not stay confined to society's fringes; it emerged from elite institutions entrusted with shaping the next generation of leaders.

Harvard, Columbia, NYU, and Berkeley became incubators for movements that justified horrific acts, including mass violence and terror, under the deceptive banner of social justice.

The allure of supporting "Palestine" has been skillfully crafted, presenting itself as a moral crusade that allows privileged Westerners to feel upright without facing real consequences. Strategic and well-funded initiatives from pro-Palestinian organizations—supported by nations like Qatar and Iran—have transformed university campuses into ideological battlegrounds, where students are mobilized into activism before grasping the complexities of the issues at hand.

Millions of dollars flow into these institutions, ensuring that 'Palestine' is presented as the defining social justice cause, while more serious conflicts elsewhere are conveniently ignored.

This phenomenon goes beyond propaganda; it reveals a more profound and more troubling reality: the persistent hatred of Jews. The rise in violent attacks on synagogues, Jewish businesses, and individuals around the world is no coincidence—it mirrors an age-old animosity that has never entirely disappeared.

At the intersection of this disturbing revival lies a dangerous alliance: the marriage of radical Islamist ideology, aimed at promoting Sharia and Islamic supremacy, with the covert antisemitism that continues to fester in segments of the Western world—a temperament that has yet to heal in the aftermath of World War II.

This unholy partnership fuels the current wave of hatred, leading to sympathy for Hamas's atrocities rather than condemnation of their actions and fostering a chilling environment in which Jewish students face ostracism on campuses. Simultaneously, pro-terrorist demonstrations are surging in cities like London, Paris, and New York.

October 7 did not bring this wave of animosity but highlighted the underlying tensions. The urgent need to confront and understand this reality cannot be overstated; it demands a critical reassessment of the narratives we support and the alliances we build to pursue justice and equity.

Only by unmasking these complexities can we hope to foster a more informed, compassionate dialogue that transcends mere activism and aligns with the pursuit of genuine, lasting peace.

October 7 didn't create this wave of hate—it revealed it.

Antisemitism, referred to as "the longest hatred," has persisted as a widespread and enduring phenomenon throughout history, taking various forms in different societies and eras. Despite extensive scholarly efforts to understand its origins and persistence, antisemitism continues to be a complex and multifaceted issue that resists simple explanation. This is prejudice.

Antisemitism has appeared in various forms throughout history, adapting to different societies' cultural and social contexts. In the ancient Greco-Roman world, Jews encountered hostility because of their monotheistic beliefs and their refusal to participate in pagan rituals, which resulted in social segregation and resentment.

With the rise of Christianity, religious antisemitism became more pronounced. Early Christian teachings portrayed Jews as responsible for the death of Jesus, leading to widespread persecution. This charge of deicide laid the groundwork for centuries of Christian antisemitism, where Jews were depicted as malevolent and in league with the devil.

During the medieval period, antisemitism took on new dimensions. Jews were frequently blamed for societal calamities, such as the Black Death, where they were accused of poisoning wells. Blood libel myths emerged, falsely alleging that Jews used the blood of Christian children in religious rituals. These unfounded accusations led to massacres and expulsions of Jewish communities across Europe.

In the modern era, antisemitism evolved yet again. The Enlightenment and the rise of secularism did not eradicate antisemitic sentiments; instead, they transformed them. Racial theories emerged, categorizing Jews as an inferior race. This racial antisemitism culminated in the horrors of the Holocaust, where the Nazis systematically exterminated six million Jews.

Challenges in Explaining the Persistence of Antisemitism

Despite many studies, scholars have had difficulty identifying a single cause for the persistence of antisemitism. Numerous theories have been proposed, each emphasizing different aspects:

Religious Explanations: Some scholars argue that religious differences, particularly the rejection of Jesus as the Messiah, have been a primary driver of antisemitism. However, this does not account for antisemitic attitudes in secular societies or among individuals without strong religious convictions.

Economic Theories: Another perspective suggests that Jews have been resented for their economic roles, either as successful merchants and financiers or, conversely, as impoverished outsiders. Yet, antisemitism has persisted in societies regardless of the financial status of Jewish communities.

Sociological Perspectives: Sociologists have examined antisemitism as a form of accusing, where Jews are blamed for societal problems. While this explains specific outbreaks of violence, it does not fully account for the deep-rooted and enduring nature of antisemitic beliefs.

These theories, while insightful, fall short of providing a comprehensive explanation. Antisemitism's adaptability— its ability to morph and persist under various pretexts— suggests that it is not rooted in any single cause but is a complex interplay of multiple factors.

Theological and Cultural Factors

One perspective suggests that antisemitism may stem from theological and cultural factors. The Hebrew Bible describes the Jews as a "chosen people," selected by God to uphold His commandments. This notion could create resentment among other groups, leading to antagonism. The Bible states: "For you are a people holy to the Lord your God. The Lord your God has chosen you out of all the peoples on the face of the earth to be his people, his treasured possession." (Deuteronomy 7:6)

Furthermore, throughout history, Jews have maintained a steadfast commitment to monotheism, resisting prevailing religious trends. They did not accept Jesus as the Messiah, leading to tensions with emerging Christian communities.

Similarly, in the 7th century, when Prophet Muhammad sought to gain Jewish followers in Medina, the Jewish tribes' refusal to recognize him as a prophet led to conflicts, resulting in battles and the eventual expulsion of Jewish tribes from the region.

This unwavering faithfulness to their faith and refusal to assimilate religiously may have contributed to perceptions of Jews as "other," fostering suspicion and hostility.

Antisemitism can also be seen as a reflection of broader societal dynamics. During times of social upheaval or economic distress, minority groups often become convenient targets. The Jews, with their unique religious and cultural practices, have frequently been portrayed in this way. This accusing mechanism serves to unify the majority against a common enemy, diverting attention from internal problems.

Moreover, the success of Jewish individuals in various fields has sometimes led to envy and resentment. This phenomenon is not unique to Jews; other minority groups, such as Asians in contemporary America, have faced similar prejudices.

In Boston, signs reading "Stop Asian Hate" have become a common sight, reflecting the growing awareness of discrimination against Asian communities. This phenomenon is particularly prominent in Boston's affluent suburbs—areas known for having some of the country's best schools and highest levels of education. However, behind this facade of awareness lies a troubling contradiction that reflects American society's complex relationship with successful minority groups.

Between "Jewton" and the Asian Community: The Story of Newton

The suburb of Newton, nicknamed "Jewton" due to its historically significant Jewish population, is a fascinating case study. In recent years, many Asian families have settled in the area, attracted by quality schools and strong community networks.

Demographic analysis shows that between 2010 and 2020, there was approximately a 35% increase in Asian residents in Newton, while the academic success rate of Asian and Jewish students in local schools consistently exceeds the national average. The latest census data indicates that these communities constitute about 25% of the suburbs' total population but represent over 40% of those with advanced degrees.

With success comes a dangerous undercurrent of resentment. These communities—Jewish and Asian—often find themselves isolated in semi-protected bubbles, admired for their achievements yet simultaneously vilified. They are accused of hoarding wealth, taking jobs, and monopolizing resources, as if their hard-earned success comes at the direct expense of others.

A 2022 Harvard University study found that 68% of Asian Americans and 73% of Jewish Americans reported experiences of discrimination in the past five years, with more than half noting that discrimination occurred in academic or professional contexts. The data points to a disturbing phenomenon: even in places where liberal values of equality and acceptance are publicly celebrated, covert discrimination often exists.

Antisemitism is a multifaceted and enduring prejudice that has adapted to various cultural, religious, and social contexts throughout history. Despite extensive scholarly efforts, a singular explanation for its persistence remains elusive. Factors such as theological differences, cultural distinctiveness, societal accusations, and economic envy have all played roles in fostering antisemitic sentiments.

Historical analysis teaches us that antisemitism has transformed over generations—from religious accusations in the Middle Ages, through economic conspiracy theories in the 19th century, to modern forms disguised as political criticism. Research published in the Journal of Contemporary Antisemitism indicates that approximately 42% of Americans hold at least one antisemitic stereotype, with the most common relating to perceptions of economic and political power.

The revival of antisemitism in its most blatant forms has starkly illuminated the world's stance toward Jewish communities in the post-Holocaust era. Recent events, particularly those that occurred on October 7, where women were victims of sexual violence, have highlighted a profound silence from prominent women's organizations and key figures.

Comprehensive documentation conducted by independent human rights researchers includes testimonies from more than 30 survivors, confirming the existence of serious sexual crimes. Nevertheless, organizations like UN Women and the #MeToo movement, which typically lead the fight against crimes against women, have remained relatively silent.

Comparative research examining various organizations' responses to global events like the October 7 massacre reveals a significant gap: while reactions to incidents of sexual violence in other conflict zones were swift and unequivocal, in this case—October 7—it took many weeks for public condemnation, which, even then, was often qualified and indecisive.

The Double Standard in Advocacy

In response to the perceived neglect of Jewish victims, a poignant slogan emerged on social media platforms: "MeToo Unless You Are a Jew." This phrase captures the frustration many feel regarding the selective application of victim advocacy. Despite United Nations investigations confirming sexual violence during the October 7 attacks, digital platforms became breeding grounds for denial and misinformation.

According to a December 2023 report by the Network Contagion Research Institute, there was a 919% increase in antisemitic content on Twitter/X and X following October

7, while Holocaust denial narratives increased by over 300%. On TikTok, content denying the sexual assaults during the attacks received millions of views, despite the UN Special Representative on Sexual Violence in Conflict, Pramila Patten, confirming "clear and convincing information" that sexual violence occurred during the attacks (UN Report, March 2024).

Dr. Tehilla Shwartz Altshuler of the Israel Democracy Institute states: "The algorithmic amplification of denial narratives on social media platforms has fostered an environment where factual information is overshadowed by politically motivated misinformation" (Journal of Digital Ethics, 2024).

Rationalization of Violence

The disturbing trend of justifying violence against Jews has emerged in numerous incidents worldwide. The November 2023 attack on Israeli football fans in Amsterdam exemplifies this troubling issue. Groups, reportedly of Moroccan descent, targeted individuals they identified as Jewish or linked to Israel, with eyewitnesses confirming that the attackers shouted "Jewish" and "IDF" during the assaults.

In the aftermath, several prominent European commentators suggested that these attacks were "understandable reactions" to the removal of a Palestinian flag in Amsterdam or to Israeli policies more broadly.

Dr. Robert Wistrich, who passed away in 2015, identified this phenomenon in his seminal work, "A Lethal Obsession: Anti-Semitism from Antiquity to the Global Jihad," noting, "The rationalization of violence against Jews represents one of the most persistent forms of antisemitism, where the victim is blamed for the violence inflicted upon them."

Former Harvard President Claudine Gay's statement that "the events did not occur in a vacuum" exemplifies what Holocaust historian Deborah Lipstadt refers to as "contextual antisemitism"—where Jewish suffering is seen as dependent on political circumstances rather than acknowledged as inherently wrong (Lipstadt, "Antisemitism Here and Now," 2019).

The Historical Record: Jewish Presence in Judea

The historical context of Jewish presence in the region now known as Israel illustrates a continuous connection lasting 3,000 years, supported by significant archaeological and historical evidence.

Archaeological discoveries at sites such as the City of David, Masada, and various other locations throughout Israel provide evidence of the ancient Jewish civilization. The Israel Antiquities Authority has documented over 6,000 sites featuring specifically Jewish artifacts that date from the Bronze Age to the Byzantine period. The Dead Sea Scrolls, discovered between 1947 and 1956, contain Jewish religious texts in Hebrew and Aramaic dating back to as early as the 3rd century BCE.

External historical accounts from various civilizations confirm the existence of the Jewish people. The Merneptah Stele (c. 1208 BCE), an Egyptian inscription, contains the earliest known reference to "Israel" outside of the Bible. The Cyrus Cylinder (539 BCE) records the decree of Persian Emperor Cyrus, permitting Jews to return to Jerusalem and rebuild their temple.

Roman historians Tacitus and Josephus extensively documented Jewish life and revolts in Judea during the 1st century CE.

Dr. Eric Cline, a Professor of Classics and Anthropology at George Washington University, states, "The archaeological evidence for a Jewish presence in ancient Judea is overwhelming and not seriously disputed by mainstream scholars" (Biblical Archaeology Review, 2020).

Roman Exile and Historical Erasure

The Roman conquest of Judea marked a pivotal moment in Jewish history. In 70 CE, after the Great Jewish Revolt (66-73 CE), Roman legions led by the future emperor Titus destroyed the Second Temple in Jerusalem. This event is commemorated by the Arch of Titus in Rome, which illustrates Roman soldiers carrying the sacred Menorah and other treasures from the Temple.

The subsequent Bar Kokhba Revolt (132-135 CE) led to Emperor Hadrian's decision to rename the province "Syria Palaestina," taking its name from the Philistines, who were historical enemies of the ancient Israelites and had disappeared centuries earlier.

Roman historian Cassius Dio noted that Hadrian "founded a city on the site of Jerusalem, which he called Aelia Capitolina," and "where the temple of their god had stood, he raised a new temple to Jupiter."

Dr. Jodi Magness, a Professor of Religious Studies at the University of North Carolina, emphasizes: "Hadrian's renaming of Judea as 'Palestine' was explicitly intended as a punitive measure to erase Jewish national identity from the land" (The Archaeology of the Holy Land, Cambridge University Press, 2021).

The Roman historian Cassius Dio reported that 580,000 Jews were killed during the Bar Kokhba revolt, with 50 fortified towns and 985 villages razed to the ground. While many Jews were killed or exiled, significant Jewish communities remained in Galilee, and Jewish life continued in Jerusalem whenever restrictions were lifted.

Continuous Jewish Presence Despite Exile

Despite Roman efforts to erase them, Jewish communities continued to flourish in the land. The Jerusalem Talmud was compiled in Tiberias during the 4th century CE, reflecting the ongoing Jewish scholarship in the region. Archaeological evidence confirms the presence of vibrant Jewish communities in Galilee, with numerous synagogues built during the Byzantine period (4th-7th centuries CE).

Medieval Jewish travelers, such as Benjamin of Tudela from the 12th century, documented established Jewish communities in Jerusalem, Tiberias, Acre, and other cities. The Cairo Geniza documents reveal extensive correspondence between Jewish communities in Egypt and various towns throughout historic Palestine during the 10th to 13th centuries.

In his comprehensive work "A History of Palestine, 634-1099," Professor Moshe Gil from Tel Aviv University documents that Jews constituted the majority of the population in many regions of the country when the Muslim conquest began in the 7th century.

Conclusion: The Danger of Selective Context

The pattern of contextualizing or justifying violence against Jews while simultaneously denying their historical connection to their ancestral homeland reveals a troubling intersection of historical pragmatism and modern issues of antisemitism.

As historian Simon Schama observes in his work "The Story of the Jews" (2014): "The denial of the Jewish historical connection to the land of Israel has evolved into a peculiar form of intellectual violence, where the very foundations of Jewish identity are subjected to scrutiny and skepticism that is not applied to any other people."

The selective application of historical context— acknowledging certain injustices while ignoring others— creates conditions that philosopher Hannah Arendt might recognize as the normalization of antisemitism in intellectual discourse.

Understanding both contemporary expressions of antisemitism and the deep historical connections of Jewish people to the land provides essential context for meaningful discussions about the complex realities of the Middle East today.

Who Were the 'Palestinians' Before 1948?

The Evolution of the Term "Palestinian"

For centuries, the term "Palestinian" did not signify a specific national identity or ethnic group. Instead, it functioned as a geographic label for anyone living in the region, irrespective of religion or ethnicity. Throughout both Ottoman rule (1517-1917) and the British Mandate (1920-1948), Jews and Arabs in the area were officially called "Palestinians."

This shared geographic identity is demonstrated by the institutions of the time:

- **The Palestine Post,** founded in 1932 by Jewish founders, served as the main English-language newspaper. It was renamed The Jerusalem Post in 1950.
- **The Palestine Symphony Orchestra** was founded in 1936 by Jewish violinist Bronislaw Huberman, uniting Jewish musicians escaping Nazi persecution in Europe.

- The **Palestine Football Association**, founded in 1928, initially consisted almost entirely of Jewish teams
- **Jews carried identity documents and passports** labeled "Palestinian," used Palestinian currency, and sent mail with Palestinian stamps

Documents from the British Mandate era consistently use "Palestinian" to refer to both Arab and Jewish residents of the region. The British census of 1922 classified individuals as "Palestinian Jews," "Palestinian Arabs," and "Palestinian Christians."

Arab Views on Palestinian Identity Before 1948

Historical records indicate that many Arab leaders dismissed the notion of a distinct Palestinian nationality during this period. Instead, they regarded the region as part of a larger Syria or as Arab land lacking specific Palestinian traits.

In testimony to the Peel Commission in 1937, Syrian leader Auni Bey Abdul-Hadi stated: "There is no such country [as Palestine]... Palestine is a term the Zionists invented... Our country was part of Syria for centuries."

The Grand Mufti of Jerusalem, Haj Amin al-Husseini, consistently referred to the region as "Southern Syria" in his writings and speeches during the 1920s and 1930s. In 1947, the Arab Higher Committee submitted a memorandum to the League of Nations that explicitly stated, "Palestine is part of Syria."

Professor Philip Hitti, a Princeton historian of Arab descent, testified before the Anglo-American Committee of Inquiry in 1946, stating, "There is no such thing as Palestine in history, absolutely not."

Even the PLO's founding charter in 1964 explicitly excluded claims to the West Bank and Gaza Strip (which were then under Jordanian and Egyptian control), focusing instead on opposing the Jewish state within the 1949 armistice lines.

Population Movements and Development

The region experienced significant demographic shifts in the late 19th and early 20th centuries. Jewish immigration increased, particularly after the First Zionist Congress in 1897 and during times of persecution in Europe. At the same time, the region also saw substantial Arab immigration. British census data indicates that the Arab population in Palestine grew significantly faster than natural birth rates. The Hope Simpson Report of 1930 noted "considerable" Arab immigration from neighboring countries. Countries were drawn by the economic development and higher wages in areas where Jews had settled.

According to records from the British Mandate, the Arab population in Palestine increased from about 660,000 in 1922 to 1.3 million in 1947—a growth rate that demographers indicate surpasses natural population growth, implying significant immigration.

The Jewish development of once-barren areas created economic opportunities that drew workers from throughout the region. C.S. Jarvis, the British Governor of the Sinai from 1922 to 1936, noted:

"The Arabs cannot be said to have capitalized on any opportunities to develop the country. They demonstrate little interest in doing so. This apparent disinterest is especially notable when considering that Arabs have historically inhabited underdeveloped areas.

Political Divisions and the Path to 1948

During the British Mandate period, distinct political movements emerged. The Jewish community established pre-state institutions, including the Jewish Agency and the Histadrut labor federation. Arab leadership, often dominated by wealthy landowning families like the Husseinis and Nashashibis, largely rejected cooperation with British authorities to develop self-governing institutions.

When the United Nations proposed its Partition Plan in 1947 (Resolution 181), which aimed to establish both a Jewish and an Arab state, the Jewish leadership accepted it, even though they received significantly less territory than they had hoped for. In contrast, the Arab leadership categorically rejected any form of Jewish self-determination.

On April 16, 1948, Jamal al-Husseini, representing the Arab Higher Committee, stated to the UN Security Council: "The Arabs did not wish for their country to be partitioned and would fight against it."

The subsequent war initiated by neighboring Arab countries and local Arab forces aimed not to establish a Palestinian state but to prevent Jewish independence and divide the territory among themselves. Egypt occupied Gaza, while Jordan invaded the West Bank, renaming it "Judea and Samaria." During the 19 years these territories were under Arab control (1948-1967), no efforts were made to establish a Palestinian state.

The Post-1967 Shift

The contemporary Palestinian national identity, as understood today, largely emerged after the 1967 Six-Day War. Before that, the West Bank had been occupied by Jordan, where residents received Jordanian citizenship, while Gaza was under Egyptian military administration.

Professor Rashid Khalidi, the Edward Said Professor of Arab Studies at Columbia University, notes in his book "Palestinian Identity: The Construction of Modern National Consciousness" (1997) that Palestinian national identity is "relatively recent" and that "Palestinian nationalism emerged during the interwar period and had to compete with Arabism and other ideologies for the loyalty of Arabs in Palestine."

Only after Israel gained control of these territories in the 1967 war—a conflict in which Israel confronted existential threats from neighboring Arab states—did calls for a distinct Palestinian state in these areas emerge prominently in international discussions.

The Palestine Liberation Organization (PLO), founded in 1964, significantly revised its charter after 1967 to emphasize the establishment of a state in the West Bank and Gaza—territories it had not previously claimed while under Arab control.

The term "Palestine" has had various meanings throughout history. It originated as a Roman creation meant to erase the Jewish connection to the land. It functioned as a geographical label under different empires without national significance and has only come to the forefront in recent decades as the basis for a distinct national identity.

The Nakba Myth

The events of 1948 represent a crucial turning point in Middle Eastern history, but the narrative surrounding these events has frequently been oversimplified. The United Nations Partition Plan (Resolution 181) sought to partition the British Mandate of Palestine into separate Jewish and Arab states, with Jerusalem under international administration. While Jewish leaders accepted this compromise despite their disappointment with the territorial restrictions, Arab leaders firmly rejected any form of Jewish self-determination in the region.

Following Israel's declaration of independence on May 14, 1948, five Arab armies—Egypt, Transjordan (now Jordan), Iraq, Syria, and Lebanon—launched a coordinated invasion. This military action transformed what could have been a political resolution into an existential conflict that would shape the region for generations.

Arab Leadership and the Palestinian Exodus

One of the most contentious aspects of this period involves the reasons behind the Palestinian Arab exodus. Conventional narratives often present this as a forced expulsion. However, primary source documents and testimonies from that time reveal a more nuanced reality frequently downplayed in contemporary discourse discussions.

Evidence from Arab Sources

Multiple Arab sources from the period acknowledge the role Arab leadership played in encouraging evacuation:

1. Khaled al-Azm, Syria's Prime Minister from 1948-49, wrote in his memoirs: "Since 1948 we have been demanding the return of the refugees to their homes. But we ourselves are the ones who encouraged them to leave... We brought disaster upon... Arab refugees, by inviting them and bringing pressure to bear upon them to leave... We have rendered them dispossessed and homeless."

2. The Jordanian newspaper Al Urdun published an article on April 9, 1953, stating: "The Arab

governments told us: 'Get out so that we can get in.'
"So we got out, but they didn't get in." The Cairo
daily Akhbar el Yom reported on October 12, 1963:
"The 15th of May, 1948, arrived... On that day, the
mufti of Jerusalem urged the Arabs of Palestine to
leave the country because the Arab armies were
about to enter and fight."

3. Haled Al Azm, who served as Syria's Prime
   Minister after the 1948 war, acknowledged in his
   1972 memoirs: "We are the ones who encouraged
   them to leave... We brought disaster upon a million
   Arab refugees by inviting them and pressuring them
   to depart."

4. Palestinian leader Mahmoud Abbas (Abu Mazen)
   wrote in the Palestinian publication Falastin al-
   Thawra in March 1976: "The Arab armies entered
   Palestine to protect the Palestinians, but instead,
   they abandoned them, forced them to leave their
   homes, and subjected them to all kinds of
   humiliation.

International Observers

Independent international observers corroborated these accounts:

1. The British newspaper The Economist reported on October 2, 1948: "Of the 62,000 Arabs who once lived in Haifa, no more than 5,000 or 6,000 remained... The most significant factors were the announcements made over the air by the Arab Higher Executive urging all Arabs to leave."
2. Time Magazine reported on May 3, 1948: "The Arabs are fleeing from Palestine by the thousands as Jewish troops advance... The Arab exodus, at least initially, was encouraged by various Arab leaders, including Haj Amin el Husseini, the exiled pro-Nazi Mufti of Jerusalem, and the Arab Higher Committee."
3. The Near East Broadcasting Station (Cyprus) reported on April 3, 1949: "It should not be overlooked that the Arab Higher Committee encouraged the refugees' departure from their homes in Jaffa, Haifa, and Jerusalem."

4. The research of historian Efraim Karsh uncovered a British intelligence report from 1948 that stated: "Arab officers ordered the complete evacuation of specific villages in certain areas, lest their inhabitants 'treacherously' acquiesce to Israeli rule or impede Arab military deployments."

Israel's Treatment of Arabs Who Remained

While hundreds of thousands of Arabs fled, around 160,000 chose to stay in Israel after the war. Rather than facing expulsion or oppression, they were granted full citizenship in the newly formed state. Today, the Arab Israeli population has grown to about two million citizens who enjoy equal rights under Israeli law, including:

- Full voting rights and representation in the Knesset (Israel's parliament).
- Arabic has been an official language of the state until 2018 and still holds special status.
- •Freedom of religion, with Islamic courts having jurisdiction over personal status matters.
- Access to education, healthcare, and social services.

- Representation in all branches of government, including the Supreme Court.

This reality sharply contrasts with the treatment of Jews in Arab countries after 1948, when around 850,000 Jews were expelled or fled from Arab nations where their communities had existed for centuries or even millennia.

The Refugee Challenge: Comparative Analysis

The Palestinian refugee situation is a unique case in world history, not due to its scale or circumstances but because of how it has been politically addressed.

Following World War II, about 12 to 14 million ethnic Germans were expelled from Eastern Europe. The 1947 Partition of India resulted in around 14 million refugees. Neither of these significantly larger refugee populations— nor any other refugee group in history—has remained in a perpetual state of refugee status across generations.

1. Only Palestinian refugees have been assigned their own dedicated UN agency (UNRWA), separate from the UN High Commissioner for Refugees (UNHCR) that manages all other refugee situations worldwide.

2. Given a definition of refugee status that uniquely passes down through generations regardless of citizenship in other countries
3. Deliberately maintained in refugee camps for over seven decades rather than being resettled

Dr. Alexander Joffe, an archaeologist and historian, asserts: "The ongoing Palestinian refugee issue arises from deliberate Arab policies designed to perpetuate the problem as a weapon against Israel and to keep Palestinians in a state of dependency."

The Historical Reality of Displacement

Even if we accept, for the sake of argument, the Palestinian narrative that Jewish forces systematically expelled Arab residents from Haifa, Jerusalem, and Tel Aviv—rather than Arab leaders urging temporary evacuation until victory—this fact alone cannot account for the conflict's persistence. Population displacement, while tragic, has been a recurring theme throughout human history. Nations rise and fall, borders shift, and communities relocate—often involuntarily.

Historical context is crucial: before the 1967 Six-Day War, the West Bank was administered by Jordan, while Gaza was under Egyptian control. During these two decades (1948-1967), neither Jordan nor Egypt established Palestinian independence in these territories. This raises a profound question:

If Palestinian sovereignty was indeed the central issue, why wasn't it prioritized when Arab nations controlled these lands? Furthermore, what accounts for the coordinated attack on Israel in 1967, when Israel did not hold any of the territories now considered essential for Palestinian statehood?

Comparative Historical Displacements

The historical record shows numerous instances of significant population displacements that did not lead to ongoing conflict:

Post-World War II European Displacements (1945-1950): Approximately 12-14 million ethnic Germans were expelled from Eastern European areas, including Poland, Czechoslovakia, and Hungary. This massive population transfer—endorsed by Allied powers at Potsdam—resulted in hundreds of thousands of deaths. However, within a generation, these communities had mainly integrated into new homes without resorting to violent efforts to reclaim lost properties.

Greek-Turkish Population Exchange (1923): After the Treaty of Lausanne, around 1.5 million people were forcibly moved—Orthodox Christians to Greece and Muslims to Turkey. Despite centuries of shared history in these areas, both nations ultimately normalized relations without clinging to generational claims to properties.

Partition of India (1947): One of history's largest population exchanges resulted in approximately 14 million Hindus, Muslims, and Sikhs being displaced across newly established borders, with casualties estimated to be between 200,000 and 2 million. While Indo-Pakistani relations remain complex, the displaced populations rebuilt their lives in new locations rather than primarily focusing on returning.

Jewish Expulsion from Arab Lands (1948-1972): Following the establishment of Israel, approximately 850,000 Jews were either expelled or fled from Arab countries where their communities had thrived for centuries. These refugees were integrated into Israel and other nations without initiating terrorist campaigns against their former homelands.

The Nature of this Conflict

What distinguishes the Israeli-Palestinian conflict is not the initial displacement—however painful and controversial—but the intentional choice to sustain the conflict rather than seek reconciliation.

While other displaced populations have rebuilt their lives and found paths to coexistence throughout history, this conflict has been marked by the weaponization of historical grievances to justify ongoing violence instead of seeking resolution.

This pattern raises more profound questions: Why have neighboring Arab nations historically maintained Palestinian refugee status across generations instead of promoting integration, as observed in other refugee crises? Why has violence against Israeli civilians been consistently portrayed as legitimate resistance rather than as a barrier to peace?

Ongoing conflict has been a deliberate choice—one supported by educational systems, political structures, and international support mechanisms that prioritize grievance over reconciliation. Even when Palestinian territories were under Arab control before 1967, attacks on Jewish communities still took place, indicating that the conflict extends beyond mere territorial claims.

The Path Forward

History demonstrates that populations can overcome even the most traumatic displacements when political structures and cultural narratives encourage reconciliation instead of revenge. The unique persistence of this conflict emphasizes not only the initial displacement but also the subsequent choices by multiple parties to maintain grievance as a central organizing principle rather than engage in the challenging yet essential work of creating a shared future.

If the narrative we often hear is true—that the conflict in the Middle East is only about a piece of land known as Israel and the Palestinians' so-called "right of return"—how do we explain the attacks on Jews when Palestine, Gaza, and the West Bank were entirely under Arab control?

The Pre-1967 Middle East Landscape

Before the Six-Day War of June 1967, the territorial situation in the Middle East presents a critical and often overlooked historical context:

The West Bank and East Jerusalem were under Jordanian control for nearly two decades (1948-1967). During this time, Jordan made no efforts to establish Palestinian self-governance or sovereignty. Similarly, Gaza remained under Egyptian administration with no meaningful steps taken toward Palestinian statehood or autonomy.

The Golan Heights, which Syria controlled, primarily served as a strategic military position where Syrian forces frequently shelled Israeli civilian communities in the Galilee. Egypt maintained control over the Sinai Peninsula, utilizing it as an army staging ground against Israel.

What is particularly significant about this historical arrangement is that Israel had no control over these territories when Arab nations initiated hostilities in 1967. This timeline fundamentally challenges the narrative that frames the conflict primarily as Israeli "occupation" of the West Bank and Gaza. The war itself illustrated that Arab opposition to Israel went beyond territorial disputes and centered on rejecting Israel's existence as a sovereign state.

The Evolution of Palestinian National Identity

The global acknowledgment of demands for a separate Palestinian state only gained significant traction after the 1967 war. Before this crucial moment, Palestinians primarily associated themselves with the broader Arab world instead of viewing themselves as a distinct national entity needing their sovereignty.

Several historical facts support this assessment:

The Palestine Liberation Organization (PLO) was established in 1964, three years before Israel gained control of the West Bank and Gaza. This timeline suggests that the organization's primary purpose could not have been about "liberating" territories that were not yet under Israeli control. Therefore, the logical conclusion is that the PLO's main objective was the elimination of Israel rather than establishing Palestinian statehood alongside it.

When Yasser Arafat became the leader of the PLO in 1969, he organized several terrorist campaigns against Israeli civilians. The PLO's charter explicitly stated the goal of destroying Israel rather than establishing a Palestinian state through peaceful coexistence.

The strategic development of a distinct Palestinian national identity appears to have been utilized as a political instrument to challenge Israel's legitimacy. PLO Executive Committee member Zahir Muhsein candidly acknowledged in a 1977 interview with the Dutch newspaper Trouw: "**The Palestinian people do not exist... the creation of a Palestinian state is simply a means to continue our struggle against Israel.**"

This remarkable admission from a senior Palestinian leader indicates that the concept of Palestinian nationhood was primarily cultivated as an anti-Israel strategy rather than arising organically from a historical nation-state tradition.

Rejected Peace Opportunities

The historical record demonstrates repeated Israeli offers of Palestinian statehood, all rejected by Palestinian leadership:

During the 2000 Camp David Summit, Israeli Prime Minister Ehud Barak presented Yasser Arafat with a comprehensive peace plan that included a Palestinian state consisting of 97% of the West Bank, all of Gaza, and East Jerusalem as its capital. Instead of continuing negotiations, Arafat rejected the proposal outright, and shortly afterward, the violence of the Second Intifada erupted.

In 2008, Israeli Prime Minister Ehud Olmert presented a more extensive proposal that included territorial land swaps to compensate for areas where Israeli settlements would remain. Palestinian Authority President Mahmoud Abbas left without even making a proposal counteroffer.

President Bill Clinton, who personally mediated the 2000 negotiations, publicly assigned responsibility for the failure to Arafat, stating unequivocally: "Arafat was here for 14 days and said no to everything." This assessment from a neutral third-party mediator carries significant weight in understanding the dynamics at play.

The Strategic Objective: Israel's Elimination

Evidence suggests Palestinian leadership has consistently prioritized Israel's destruction above Palestinian sovereignty or economic development:

Hamas's governing charter explicitly states: "Israel will exist and will continue to exist until Islam obliterates it." This foundational document makes no pretense about seeking peaceful coexistence.

Israel's total withdrawal from Gaza in 2005 created a clear opportunity to foster autonomous Palestinian governance and civil society. Instead, Hamas seized control and diverted international humanitarian resources toward military infrastructure, tunnel networks, and rocket manufacturing rather than economic development.

The Broader Historical Context

Historical evidence shows that Israel has consistently demonstrated a willingness to make painful territorial concessions for the sake of peace. The primary obstacle has been the Palestinian leadership's ideological commitment to eliminating Israel rather than accepting a Jewish state within any borders.

If establishing Palestinian sovereignty were the primary goal, the numerous generous offers would have laid the groundwork for a state. Instead, these chances were consistently turned down in favor of ongoing conflict.

The uncomfortable conclusion is that Palestinian political leadership—supported by regional powers promoting radical ideologies—has consistently prioritized anti-Israel sentiment over real improvements in Palestinian living conditions and governance. This pattern suggests that the conflict endures not due to a lack of viable solutions, but rather because of a strategic choice to sustain it.

The UN Partition Plan (1947): A Rejected Opportunity

The 1947 United Nations Partition Plan marked a historic turning point in the Middle East. Resolution 181 suggested dividing the British Mandate of Palestine into separate Jewish and Arab states—a pragmatic solution recognizing both peoples' claims to the land.

Despite receiving significantly less territory than they had hoped for, the Jewish leadership accepted this compromise to establish sovereignty and promote peace and coexistence.

In stark contrast, Arab leadership firmly rejected the two-state solution. Instead of engaging with the proposal or providing constructive alternatives, they responded with a coordinated military campaign against the emerging Israeli state. This rejection established a pattern that would recur throughout the conflict's history: Palestinian leadership consistently chose confrontation over compromise when faced with opportunities for coexistence.

This initial rejection holds profound historical significance. If Arab leaders had accepted the partition plan, a Palestinian state could have existed since 1948, sparing generations from the subsequent conflict. Instead, the choice to pursue Israel's elimination through military means triggered decades of instability and suffering.

A Consistent Strategy of Terror (1948-Present)

Since Israel's establishment, Palestinian organizations have used terrorism as a key political tool. This strategy has resulted in attacks aimed explicitly at civilians rather than military targets, reflecting a deliberate policy of utilizing civilian casualties to further political objectives.

Notable Attacks Highlighting This Pattern:

The 1972 Munich Olympics Massacre: The Black September organization infiltrated the Olympic Village, killing two Israeli athletes immediately and taking nine others hostage. All hostages were eventually murdered during a failed rescue attempt. This attack, broadcast globally, demonstrated the willingness to target civilians on an international stage.

The 1985 Achille Lauro Hijacking: Members of the Palestine Liberation Front hijacked an Italian cruise ship carrying over 400 passengers. During this hostage crisis, they singled out Leon Klinghoffer, a 69-year-old wheelchair-bound American Jewish passenger, shooting him and throwing his body overboard. This act of targeting a defenseless elderly civilian exemplified the brutal nature of these tactics.

The Second Intifada Campaign (2000-2005): Following the rejection of peace proposals at Camp David, Palestinian leadership orchestrated a wave of suicide bombings targeting Israeli civilian centers. The 2001 Dolphinarium attack specifically targeted a Tel Aviv nightclub popular with teenagers, killing 21 young people and injuring over

100 more. This deliberate targeting of youth venues represented an alarming escalation.

Strategic Kidnappings: The 2006 abduction of Israeli soldier Gilad Shalit, who was held captive for five years in harsh conditions, exemplified another tactic. His eventual release required Israel to free over 1,000 Palestinian prisoners, many of whom were convicted of terrorism, setting a precedent that encouraged further kidnappings.

Systematic Bus Bombings: Throughout the 1990s and early 2000s, Palestinian terrorist groups executed a coordinated campaign targeting public transportation. These attacks were specifically designed to maximize civilian casualties in confined spaces where escape was nearly impossible. The psychological impact extended beyond the immediate fatalities, instilling widespread fear concerning routine daily activities.

This consistent pattern of targeting civilians instead of military objectives separates these actions from legitimate resistance movements. International law explicitly prohibits the deliberate targeting of civilian populations, regardless of political grievances.

The Sustained Rocket Campaign: Psychological Warfare Against Civilians

For over twenty years, Israeli communities near the Gaza Strip have faced systematic rocket attacks from Hamas and other Palestinian groups. This campaign is a deliberate strategy of psychological warfare against civilian populations.

Since 2001, thousands of rockets have been fired indiscriminately toward Israeli towns and cities. The communities within range experience a fundamentally altered reality:

Constant Psychological Pressure: In border towns like Sderot, residents know they may have just 15 seconds to reach shelter when sirens sound. This ongoing threat fosters a state of hypervigilance that results in significant psychological trauma. Clinical studies have shown notably higher rates of post-traumatic stress disorder, anxiety disorders, and depression among residents in areas affected by rockets.

Childhood Development Under Fire: Children raised in these communities encounter developmental challenges directly connected to security issues. Many exhibit heightened startle responses, sleep disturbances, regression in developmental milestones, and difficulties concentrating in educational settings. Pediatric mental health services indicate that typical childhood experiences are often disrupted by security incidents, resulting in a generation whose formative years are defined by conflict.

Education Under Barrier: Academic institutions across southern Israel have had to adapt to the reality of rocket threats. Schools are designed with reinforced safe rooms, and security drills are as routine as academic lessons. Studies have shown lower educational achievement and higher dropout rates in areas most impacted by rocket fire, highlighting the long-term societal effects of this campaign.

Economic Destabilization: The economic consequences extend beyond immediate physical damage. During heightened tension, businesses in affected regions face increased insurance costs, workforce disruptions, and reduced consumer traffic. Agricultural activities—the economic backbone of many border communities—suffer significantly. Risky endeavors, with farmers often compelled to abandon their fields during security incidents.

What distinguishes this confrontation from traditional warfare is its deliberate targeting of civilian areas that lack military significance. The rockets are unguided weapons that cannot be aimed at specific military targets, making them inherently indiscriminate. Their military effectiveness is limited, while their psychological impact is heightened—showing their primary function as instruments of terror rather than conventional military aims.

Historical Pattern and Contemporary Implications

The consistent rejection of compromise solutions—from the 1947 Partition Plan to the Camp David and Taba negotiations—coupled with the ongoing campaign of violence against civilians reveals a troubling historical pattern. Palestinian leadership has consistently chosen maximalist positions and violent tactics instead of pursuing negotiated solutions that could have established sovereignty and improved living conditions for their people.

This pattern indicates that the conflict continues not due to a lack of viable solutions but rather from a strategic choice to sustain it. The refusal to acknowledge Israel's existence—regardless of its borders—has been the primary barrier to peace, causing ongoing suffering on both sides and obstructing the creation of a Palestinian state that could have been established for decades.

Understanding this historical context is crucial for any meaningful assessment of the current situation. Peace requires leadership that embraces compromise and coexistence rather than pursuing maximalist goals through violence.

The historical record indicates that such leadership has consistently been lacking on the Palestinian side. This explains why multiple generations have grown up without the resolution that could have been reached by accepting the numerous peace proposals presented throughout the conflict's history.

The Strategy of Violence

The horrific events of October 7, 2023, during the Jewish holiday of Sukkot, signify the tragic peak of decades of terror. On that morning, Hamas terrorists breached Israel's borders and systematically targeted civilian communities, mainly focusing on Israelis who had been the most vocal advocates for Palestinian development and humanitarian assistance. This cruel irony underscores the fundamental disconnect between Hamas's actions and any legitimate path to Palestinian prosperity.

What unfolded that day defies comprehension: a coordinated campaign of indiscriminate murder, sexual violence, kidnapping, and brutality on a scale unprecedented in Israel's history since the holocaust.

Women were subjected to sexual assault in front of their families. Children were executed in their beds. Entire families were systematically eliminated—their homes transformed from sanctuaries to crime scenes in a matter of minutes. The elderly and disabled were shown no mercy. These were not military targets; they were civilian populations deliberately selected for maximum psychological impact.

The Rejection of Coexistence

This attack occurred against a backdrop of significant Israeli and international investment in Gaza's development. For years, Israel had facilitated:

- Regular medical treatment for Gazans in Israeli hospitals, including complex pediatric care unavailable in Gaza

- Employment permits allowing thousands of Gazans to work in Israel, providing crucial economic support for Gaza families
- Transfer of humanitarian aid, including food, medicine, and building materials
- Infrastructure development, including electricity and water systems
- Agricultural expertise and training programs

These initiatives represented concrete efforts toward normalization and coexistence. Yet, Hamas's response was to weaponize these connections, exploiting the familiarity with Israeli communities gained through work permits to plan their attack and using humanitarian crossing points as infiltration routes.

October 7 demonstrated that Hamas's goal was never about Palestinian prosperity or a two-state solution—it was, as their charter explicitly states, the destruction of Israel, regardless of the cost to Palestinian civilians.

The Crucial Question: What Has Violence Achieved?

The most penetrating question that must be addressed concerns results: What has this decades-long campaign of violence achieved for the Palestinian people?

After thousands of rocket attacks, countless terror operations, suicide bombings, and now the massacre on October 7, what tangible benefits have accrued to ordinary people? Palestinians? An honest assessment reveals a devastating reality:

Economic Devastation: Gaza's economy has been systematically devastated—not solely by Israeli actions, but by Hamas's prioritization of military infrastructure over civilian development. International aid bills have been redirected toward tunnel networks and weapons acquisition instead of infrastructure for schools and hospitals.

Humanitarian Regression: By most measures—access to education, healthcare, economic opportunities, and essential services—conditions for Palestinians have worsened instead of improved under Hamas governance.

Security Constraints: The predictable Israeli security responses to terror attacks have led to restrictions that complicate daily life for Palestinians—border closures, checkpoints, and security barriers that would be unnecessary in a context of peaceful coexistence.

The undeniable conclusion is that violence has achieved precisely the opposite of what would benefit the Palestinian population. Israel remains strong and resolute, while conditions for Palestinians continue to deteriorate with each escalation.

The Cycle of Self-Destructive Decision Making

The events of October 7 exemplify this pattern of self-destructive decision-making. Hamas leadership understood with complete certainty that their actions would provoke a massive Israeli military response. They were aware their attack would lead to:

1. The immediate closure of border crossings that had permitted thousands of Gazans to work in Israel.
2. The suspension of humanitarian aid flows.

3. A military campaign that would inevitably damage Gaza's infrastructure.
4. International isolation as the world witnessed their atrocities.

Yet they proceeded anyway—a choice that can only be justified by placing ideological goals above the well-being of their people. This embodies the opposite of responsible governance.

The ancient wisdom rings true: "Insanity is doing the same thing repeatedly and expecting different results." Hamas has launched terror campaigns against Israel for decades, and each time, the outcome has been the same: increased suffering for Palestinians without furthering their stated political goals.

The Incomprehensible International Response

Perhaps the most puzzling is the international community's response to this pattern. Despite irrefutable evidence of Hamas's responsibility for Palestinian suffering—ranging from their diversion of humanitarian resources to terror infrastructure and their use of civilian facilities as military installations—a considerable portion of global opinion continues to blame Israel primarily.

This misattribution of responsibility creates a twisted incentive structure that rewards terrorist governance and punishes democratic responses to terror. When Hamas launches rockets from schools and hospitals, deliberately endangering Palestinian civilians, international criticism often targets Israel's reaction rather than the initial violation of international law.

This distorted perception only prolongs the suffering of Palestinians by validating Hamas's leadership and tactics. It reinforces a governance model that has repeatedly failed its population while providing no viable path to statehood or prosperity.

The Painful Truth

The uncomfortable reality we must acknowledge is that Hamas has emerged as the most significant barrier to Palestinian progress. Their governance model has led to poverty, isolation, and violence while failing to achieve any meaningful advances toward Palestinian statehood or better living conditions.

The October 7 attack and its aftermath have once again highlighted the ineffectiveness of Hamas's approach. The devastation in Gaza—the destroyed homes, disrupted lives, and shattered communities—stems directly from Hamas's choice to prioritize Israel's destruction over Palestinian well-being.

Until the international community consistently recognizes this dynamic and holds Hamas accountable for its governance failures and human rights violations, Palestinians will remain caught in this cycle of violence. Peace cannot arise from terror; prosperity cannot be built on a foundation of hatred.

The way forward necessitates Palestinian leadership dedicated to true state-building instead of ongoing conflict—leadership that prioritizes Palestinian welfare as the primary goal rather than a secondary concern in an ideological battle. Only when such leadership arises can Palestinians start to create the future they deserve.

The Weight of Knowledge in the Face of Hatred

As I conclude this exploration of historical truth, I must acknowledge the profound difficulties we face as Israelis and Jews. There is a particular burden in knowing these historical realities while simultaneously confronting waves of hatred and misinformation from organizations and individuals who have never experienced our lived experiences.

The institutional bias against Israel has manifested in troubling ways within international bodies that were established to promote peace and justice. The United Nations, for instance, has passed more resolutions condemning Israel than all other nations combined—a statistical anomaly that cannot be explained by objective assessment. In 2022 alone, the UN General Assembly adopted 15 resolutions singling out Israel while passing only 13 resolutions on the rest of the world combined.

UN bodies such as the Human Rights Council have shown systematic bias, as Israel is the only country with a permanent agenda item focused on its criticism. At the same time, the United Nations Relief and Works Agency (UNRWA) has continued to uphold the refugee status of

Palestinians across generations—a practice applied to no other refugee population in the world—while numerous UNRWA employees have been implicated in promoting antisemitism and even participating in terrorist activities. Perhaps the most painful aspect is the deliberate erasure of Jewish history by UNESCO, which has passed resolutions denying Jewish connections to our most sacred sites, including the Temple Mount and the Western Wall in Jerusalem. These aren't just political positions—they represent an attempt to delegitimize our very existence and historical connection to our homeland.

Personal Attacks and Historical Distortions

The hostility extends beyond institutions and seeps into everyday online interactions, where sharing even basic historical facts can provoke immediate personal attacks. Every video I post receives dismissive comments that label me as a "Polish Jew trying to teach them about the region"—a statement demonstrating a profound ignorance of both Israeli society and Jewish history.

These commenters fail to recognize that Israeli Jews embody a rich textile of backgrounds. While some certainly have European ancestry, others have deep historical ties to the Middle East and North Africa. Approximately 850,000 Jews were expelled from Arab countries after Israel's establishment—communities that had flourished for centuries in Iraq, Yemen, Egypt, Morocco, and other nations throughout the region.

My own family history illustrates this diversity. Genetic testing confirms that my lineage traces back to the Bene Moshe tribe, descendants of ancient Judean communities who, after conquest and exile, migrated to the area near Bombay, India. My ancestors upheld Jewish traditions and practices for generations despite living thousands of miles from Jerusalem. Following the establishment of Israel, they returned to their ancestral homeland—completing a historical circle that spans millennia rather than decades.

The scientific evidence is clear: DNA studies consistently demonstrate the genetic continuity between modern Jewish populations and ancient Levantine peoples. These findings have been published in esteemed journals such as Nature and the American Journal of Human Genetics, reinforcing our cultural memory—that regardless of where the diaspora has taken us, our roots remain in this land.

The casual dismissal of these historical and scientific realities by online commenters who favor convenient narratives over documented facts is frustrating and sad. It reflects a willful ignorance that renders meaningful dialogue nearly impossible.

Finding Hope in Unity

Yet, despite these challenges, I find myself unexpectedly hopeful. The aftermath of October 7 has revealed something profound about our people—a capacity for unity and mutual support that transcends political differences and geographical boundaries.

The solidarity I've witnessed among Israelis and Jews worldwide since that terrible day has been nothing short of transformative. Communities that once seemed divided by political perspectives, religious observance, or cultural expressions have come together with a shared sense of purpose and compassion.

I've seen secular residents of Tel Aviv opening their homes to families evacuated from the north and south. I've witnessed Haredi and Reform Jews standing side by side at rallies, demanding the return of hostages. I've experienced the outpouring of support from Jewish communities across the diaspora—providing not just material aid but also standing proudly and publicly with Israel in the face of intimidation and threats.

This unity stems not from political convenience or superficial sentiment but from a profound reservoir of shared identity and values. It reminds us that beneath our disagreements lies a fundamental connection that external forces or internal disputes cannot sever.

The Hebrew phrase "Kol Yisrael arevim zeh lazeh" (All Israel is responsible for one another) has renewed significance in these challenging months. When terrorists attacked on October 7, they did not differentiate between religious and secular, left-wing and right-wing, Ashkenazi and Sephardi—they targeted Jews. In response, we have found that our shared identity is more powerful than our differences.

This solidarity presents a model for healing not only within Jewish communities but also for broader reconciliation. It shows that even after experiencing traumatic violence, our human capacity for connection and mutual support remains our greatest strength.

Final Thoughts: Seeking Truth in a Complex World

Thank you for taking the time to read this book. In an age when narratives are well-curated, and history is often distorted, we must pursue knowledge, challenge assumptions, and consider all perspectives before forming an opinion. The conflicts we discuss are not merely theoretical; they shape real lives, influence policies, and carry significant consequences.

I invite you to continue this journey of understanding. If my words resonate, I encourage you to explore "6 Million and a Day." My collection of poetry and art explores the unimaginable pain and resilience of the Jewish people after October 7.

Much love, Yama.

6 Million and a Day

Bibliography

American Jewish Committee (AJC). n.d. "Israel Conflict Timeline." https://www.ajc.org/IsraelConflictTimeline.

Britannica. n.d. "Arab Israeli War of 1948." https://www.britannica.com.

Cambridge University Press. n.d. *Israel's Moment: US and UN Arms Embargo, November 1947–May 1948.* https://www.cambridge.org.

De Gruyter. n.d. "Israel and the Middle East." https://www.degruyter.com.

Encyclopedia of the Holocaust. n.d. "History of Antisemitism." United States Holocaust Memorial Museum. https://encyclopedia.ushmm.org.

Institute for the Study of Global Antisemitism and Policy (ISGAP). n.d. "Research on Antisemitism in Academia." https://isgap.org.

Jewish Virtual Library. n.d. "History of the Israeli-Palestinian Conflict." https://www.jewishvirtuallibrary.org.

Jewish Post. n.d. "Middle East Analysis." https://www.jewishpost.com.

The Jerusalem Post. n.d. "News and Analysis." https://www.jpost.com.

Times of Israel. n.d. "Blogs and Opinion Pieces." https://blogs.timesofisrael.com.

United Nations. n.d. "UNISPAL: History of the Israeli-Palestinian Conflict." https://www.un.org/unispal/history/.

United States Department of State. n.d. "The 1948 Arab-Israeli War." https://history.state.gov/milestones/1945-1952/arab-israeli-war.

The JC (Jewish Chronicle). n.d. "Investigative Reports on Middle East Affairs." https://www.thejc.com.

National Association of Scholars (NAS). n.d. "Outsourced to Qatar: A Case Study of Northwestern University Qatar." https://www.nas.org/blogs/event/outsourced-to-qatar-a-case-study-of-northwestern-university-qatar.

Wikipedia. n.d. "1948 Arab Israeli War." https://en.wikipedia.org/wiki/1948_Arab%E2%80%93Israeli_War.

U.S. Census Bureau. 2020. *Demographics Report for Newton, Massachusetts.*

Harvard University Study on Discrimination Experiences. 2022.

Journal of Contemporary Antisemitism. 2023. "Modern Manifestations of Antisemitism in America."

Pew Research Center. 2023. "Attitudes Toward Discrimination and Prejudice."

Human Rights Watch. 2023. *Documentation of Gender-Based Violence in Conflict Zones.*

Anti-Defamation League. 2022. *Annual Audit of Antisemitic Incidents.*

Printed in Dunstable, United Kingdom

70130841R00077